ISSUES THAT CONCERN YOU

Anxiety
Disorders

Brian Kennedy, *Book Editor*

GREENHAVEN PRESS
A part of Gale, Cengage Learning

GALE
CENGAGE Learning·

Detroit • New York • San Francisco • New Haven, Conn • Waterville, Maine • London

Christine Nasso, *Publisher*
Elizabeth Des Chenes, *Managing Editor*

For more information, contact:
Greenhaven Press
27500 Drake Rd.
Farmington Hills, MI 48331-3535
Or you can visit our Internet site at gale.cengage.com

Articles in Greenhaven Press anthologies are often edited for length to meet page requirements. In addition, original titles of these works are changed to clearly present the main thesis and to explicitly indicate the author's opinion. Every effort is made to ensure that Greenhaven Press accurately reflects the original intent of the authors. Every effort has been made to trace the owners of copyrighted material.

Cover image copyright Monkey Business Images, 2009. Used under license from Shutterstock.com.

LIBRARY OF CONGRESS CATALOGING-IN-PUBLICATION DATA

Anxiety disorders / Brian Kennedy, book editor.
   p. cm. -- (Issues that concern you)
 Includes bibliographical references and index.
 ISBN 978-0-7377-4743-0 (hardcover)
 1. Anxiety. 2. Teenagers--Mental health--United States. I. Kennedy, Brian, 1978–
  BF575.A6A585 2010
  618.92'8522--dc22

                                 2009043385

Printed in the United States of America
2 3 4 5 6 7 14 13 12 11 10

CONTENTS

INTRODUCTION

Everyone deals with stress and anxiety at certain times. New experiences, important tests, or moving away from home can make anyone nervous. Indeed, a certain level of anxiety is often healthy: It is the fear that tells us not to get too close to a wild animal or the edge of a cliff. But too much anxiety is unhealthy. For those with anxiety disorders, anxiety can control their lives, prevent them from functioning normally, and cause other physical symptoms. These problems have existed for thousands of years but have only recently been recognized as independent diagnoses—in 1980 the American Psychiatric Association first listed the current definitions of anxiety disorders in the *Diagnostic and Statistical Manual of Mental Disorders III (DSM-III)*. In the years since, awareness of anxiety disorders has grown. More research is being conducted into causes and treatments, and high-profile cases such as those of NFL player Ricky Williams (social anxiety disorder), singer Carly Simon (panic attacks), and fictional TV detective Adrian Monk (obsessive-compulsive disorder), are raising awareness about this wide-ranging problem.

Anxiety disorders are the most common mental disorders in America, affecting as many as 40 million people. The term "anxiety disorders" includes a wide range of conditions, but they are all characterized by extreme anxiety and mood or emotional disturbances. Anxiety disorders include specific phobias, which are particularized fears of an object or situation (for example, snakes, heights, or water), exposure to which causes extreme anxiety and possibly panic attacks. Generalized anxiety disorder (GAD) is a more unfocused, pervasive anxiety, causing fatigue, insomnia, and other health problems. Social anxiety disorder (SAD), or social phobia, is an unreasonable and overwhelming fear of social situations. Those with SAD avoid socializing and have difficulty interacting with others in social and work settings. The fear that others may notice the condition often worsens it.

Obsessive-compulsive disorder (OCD) is characterized by obsessive thoughts and anxiety, nagging doubt, and the need to have things in order. A common manifestation is an obsession with germs and cleanliness, marked by repetitive hand washing. Sufferers are aware of the seemingly absurd nature of their conduct but are powerless to control it. "It's called 'insanity with insight' or 'the doubting disease,'" says Bruce Hyman of the OCD Resource Center of South Florida. "It is a living hell for those who have it."

Post-traumatic stress disorder (PTSD) is caused by a traumatic event, such as rape, assault, a natural disaster, an accident, or abuse. It is also common in soldiers returning from war. Symptoms may include flashbacks, nightmares, insomnia, and anger.

Separation anxiety is most commonly triggered when young children are away from their parents; it affects the children and the parents alike. Moving away to college can also cause separation anxiety. Leaving lifelong friendships is difficult, says Jennifer Crissman Ishler, assistant professor of counselor education at Pennsylvania State University: "This loss and separation often trigger emotional distress resulting in adjustment difficulties." New research also indicates that separation anxiety is common in pets, often accounting for unruly and disruptive behavior when left alone or in the care of others.

Anxiety disorders often coexist with other problems. For instance, as many as two-thirds of those with generalized anxiety disorder will also battle depression. Anxiety sufferers are also at increased risk of alcohol and drug abuse. In a paper published in the *Archives of General Psychiatry*, Bridget F. Grant from the National Institutes of Health explains, "Numerous clinical studies consistently indicate that substance use disorders and mood and anxiety disorders have strong associations." Additionally, many people with one anxiety disorder are often later diagnosed with additional anxiety disorders.

Many cases of anxiety disorders go unreported and therefore untreated. People often do not realize they have problems; they believe they are just high-stressed, not that they suffer from a recognized condition. Others are ashamed to admit they have problems or to seek treatment, fearing the stigma they perceive to be attached to mental disorders. This has been particularly problematic in the military, where soldiers feel they will be seen as weak should they seek treatment for PTSD. The *Psychiatric Times* reports that many veterans who screen positive for disorders do not receive treatment, often citing fear of "perceptions that they would be labeled 'crazy' and that there might be negative consequences for their military career." When left untreated, PTSD can lead to violence, substance abuse, and depression.

Many of the historical methods used to treat anxiety disorders now seem ridiculous. Bathing in extremely cold rivers, bloodletting

Antianxiety drugs have grown into a major industry. Effexor alone generated $3.7 billion in sales in 2006.

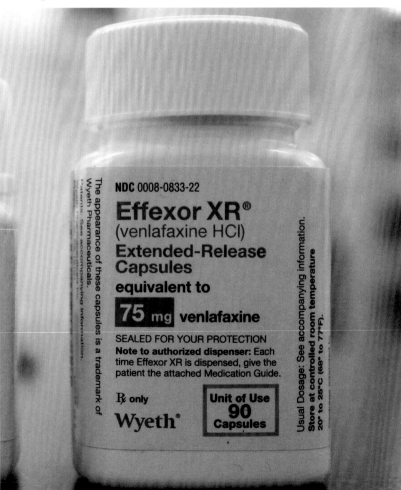

(by applying leeches to the body), and exposing patients to extreme temperatures were all, at one time, used as treatments. Today, a variety of more modern treatment options is available. Perhaps the most common is medication. Antianxiety drugs have been around for decades, and prescription anxiety pills have grown into a major industry. For instance, Effexor, a drug used to treat anxiety and depression, generated $3.7 billion in sales in 2006. However, many experts are concerned over the abuse of these medications, as people with normal levels of anxiety—not disorders—are obtaining prescription medications.

Counseling is another treatment method and can help patients deal with a variety of disorders, including phobias and PTSD. Cognitive-behavioral therapy (CBT) is a form of treatment that focuses on both thought patterns (the "cognitive" aspect) and responses to problematic situations (the "behavioral" aspect), the combination of which can help sufferers confront and overcome anxiety disorders. Another technique for treating phobias and OCD involves a gradual exposure to the fear. This process, known as systematic desensitization, helps people overcome their problems by teaching them relaxation skills and having them confront their fears head-on. Alternative remedies are also available: Meditation, acupuncture, and herbal medicines are all used to treat anxiety. Diet and exercise can often lower anxiety levels, especially when used in conjunction with other treatment methods.

This anthology considers the variety of anxiety disorders and their impacts on both individuals and society. Additionally, these magazine articles, news reports, and excerpts from other sources discuss treatment options, both historical and modern. A thorough bibliography lists both books and articles for additional reading, and a list of organizations provides contacts for extra information. In the appendix, "What You Should Know About Anxiety Disorders" lists important facts and statistics for quick reference, and "What You Should Do About Anxiety Disorders" offers advice on understanding the issue and how to cope should you or someone close to you suffer from such a disorder. *Issues That Concern You: Anxiety Disorders* is an excellent resource and a great starting point for anyone interested in this important issue.

ONE

Anxiety Disorders: An Overview

Office of the Surgeon General

> The report from the U.S. surgeon general's office excerpted in this viewpoint is a collaboration of two U.S. governmental agencies: the Substance Abuse and Mental Health Services Administration (SAMHSA) and the National Institute of Mental Health (NIMH). The report was created to promote the awareness, understanding, and treatment of mental health disorders in the United States. It explains how anxiety disorders are the most common mental disorders and provides general information and statistics about each specific type of anxiety disorder, including definitions, causes, symptoms, treatments, and prevalence.

The anxiety disorders are the most common, or frequently occurring, mental disorders. They encompass a group of conditions that share extreme or pathological [habitual or compulsive] anxiety as the principal disturbance of mood or emotional tone. Anxiety, which may be understood as the pathological counterpart of normal fear, is manifest by disturbances of mood, as well as of thinking, behavior, and physiological activity.

Office of the Surgeon General, "Adults and Mental Health: Anxiety Disorders," *Mental Health: A Report of the Surgeon General.* Rockville, MD: U.S. Department of Health and Human Services, 1999.

Types of Anxiety Disorders

The anxiety disorders include panic disorder (with and without a history of agoraphobia), agoraphobia (with and without a history of panic disorder), generalized anxiety disorder, specific phobia, social phobia, obsessive-compulsive disorder, acute stress disorder, and post-traumatic stress disorder. In addition, there are adjustment disorders with anxious features, anxiety disorders due to general medical conditions, substance-induced anxiety disorders, and the residual category of anxiety disorder not otherwise specified.

Anxiety disorders not only are common in the United States, but they are ubiquitous [everywhere] across human cultures. In the United States, 1-year prevalence for all anxiety disorders among adults ages 18 to 54 exceeds 16 percent and there is significant overlap or comorbidity [coexistence] with mood and substance abuse disorders. . . . Although few psychological autopsy studies of adult suicides have included a focus on comorbid conditions, it is likely that the rate of comorbid anxiety in suicide is underestimated. Panic disorder and agoraphobia, particularly, are associated with increased risks of attempted suicide.

Panic Attacks and Panic Disorder

A panic attack is a discrete [distinct] period of intense fear or discomfort that is associated with numerous somatic [physical] and cognitive [mental] symptoms. These symptoms include palpitations, sweating, trembling, shortness of breath, sensations of choking or smothering, chest pain, nausea or gastrointestinal distress, dizziness or lightheadedness, tingling sensations, and chills or blushing and "hot flashes." The attack typically has an abrupt onset, building to maximum intensity within 10 to 15 minutes. Most people report a fear of dying, "going crazy," or losing control of emotions or behavior. The experiences generally provoke a strong urge to escape or flee the place where the attack begins and, when associated with chest pain or shortness of breath, frequently results in seeking aid from a hospital emergency room or other type of urgent assistance. Yet an attack rarely lasts longer than 30 minutes. . . . The panic attack is distinguished from other forms of anxiety by its intensity and its sudden, episodic nature. Panic attacks may be further characterized by the relationship between the onset of the attack and the presence or absence of situational factors. . . .

Panic attacks are not always indicative of a mental disorder, and up to 10 percent of otherwise healthy people experience an

Panic disorder is diagnosed when a person experiences panic attacks, has a fear of having more attacks, and changes behavior to minimize incidents.

isolated panic attack per year. Panic attacks also are not limited to panic disorder. They commonly occur in the course of social phobia, generalized anxiety disorder, and major depressive disorder.

Panic disorder is diagnosed when a person has experienced at least two unexpected panic attacks *and* develops persistent concern or worry about having further attacks or changes his or her behavior to avoid or minimize such attacks. Whereas the number and severity of the attacks varies widely, the concern and avoidance behavior are essential features. The diagnosis is inapplicable when the attacks are presumed to be caused by a drug or medication or a general medical disorder, such as hyperthyroidism. . . .

Panic disorder is about twice as common among women as men. Age of onset is most common between late adolescence and midadult life, with onset relatively uncommon past age 50. . . .

Agoraphobia

The ancient term agoraphobia is translated from Greek as fear of an open marketplace. Agoraphobia today describes severe and pervasive anxiety about being in situations from which escape might be difficult or avoidance of situations such as being alone outside of the home, traveling in a car, bus, or airplane, or being in a crowded area.

Most people who present to mental health specialists develop agoraphobia after the onset of panic disorder. Agoraphobia is best understood as an adverse behavioral outcome of repeated panic attacks and the subsequent worry, preoccupation, and avoidance. . . .

Agoraphobia occurs about two times more commonly among women than men. The gender difference may be attributable to social-cultural factors that encourage, or permit, the greater expression of avoidant coping strategies by women, although other explanations are possible.

Specific Phobias

These common conditions are characterized by marked fear of specific objects or situations. Exposure to the object of the phobia, either in real life or via imagination or video, invariably elicits intense anxiety, which may include a (situationally bound) panic attack. Adults generally recognize that this intense fear is irrational. Nevertheless, they typically avoid the phobic stimulus or endure exposure with great difficulty. The most common specific phobias include the following feared stimuli or situations: animals (especially snakes, rodents, birds, and dogs); insects (especially spiders and bees or hornets); heights; elevators; flying; automobile driving; water; storms; and blood or injections.

Approximately 8 percent of the adult population suffers from one or more specific phobias in 1 year. Much higher rates would be recorded if less rigorous diagnostic requirements for avoidance or functional impairment were employed. Typically, the specific phobias begin in childhood, although there is a second "peak" of onset in the middle 20s of adulthood. Most phobias persist for years or even decades, and relatively few remit spontaneously or without treatment.

The specific phobias generally do not result from exposure to a single traumatic event (i.e., being bitten by a dog or nearly drowning). Rather, there is evidence of phobia in other family members and social or vicarious learning of phobias. Spontaneous, unexpected panic attacks also appear to play a role in the development of specific phobias, although the particular pattern of avoidance is much more focal and circumscribed.

Social Phobia

Social phobia, also known as social anxiety disorder, describes people with marked and persistent anxiety in social situations, including performances and public speaking. The critical element of the fearfulness is the possibility of embarrassment or ridicule. Like specific phobias, the fear is recognized by adults as excessive or unreasonable, but the dreaded social situation is avoided or is tolerated with great discomfort. Many people with social phobia are preoccupied with concerns that others will see their anxiety symptoms (i.e., trembling, sweating, or blushing); or notice their halting or rapid speech; or judge them to be weak, stupid, or "crazy." Fears of fainting, losing control of bowel or bladder function, or having one's mind going blank are also not uncommon. Social phobias generally are associated with significant anticipatory anxiety for days or weeks before the dreaded event, which in turn may further handicap performance and heighten embarrassment. . . .

Social phobia is more common in women. Social phobia typically begins in childhood or adolescence and, for many, it is associated with the traits of shyness and social inhibition. A public humiliation, severe embarrassment, or other stressful experience may provoke an intensification of difficulties. Once the disorder is established, complete remissions are uncommon without treatment. More commonly, the severity of symptoms and impairments tends to fluctuate in relation to vocational demands and the stability of social relationships. Preliminary data suggest social phobia to be familial [run in families].

Generalized Anxiety Disorder

Generalized anxiety disorder is defined by a protracted (greater than 6 months' duration) period of anxiety and worry, accompanied by multiple associated symptoms. These symptoms include muscle tension, easy fatiguability, poor concentration, insomnia, and irritability. In youth, the condition is known as overanxious disorder of childhood. . . . An essential feature of generalized anxiety disorder is that the anxiety and worry cannot be attributable to the more focal distress of panic disorder, social phobia, obsessive-compulsive disorder, or other conditions. Rather, as implied by the name, the excessive worries often pertain to many areas, including work, relationships, finances, the well-being of one's family, potential misfortunes, and impending deadlines. Somatic anxiety symptoms are common, as are sporadic panic attacks.

Generalized anxiety disorder occurs more often in women, with a sex ratio of about 2 women to 1 man. . . . Approximately 50 percent of cases begin in childhood or adolescence. The disorder typically runs a fluctuating course, with periods of increased symptoms usually associated with life stress or impending difficulties.

There does not appear to be a specific familial association for general anxiety disorder. Rather, rates of other mood and anxiety disorders typically are greater among first-degree relatives of people with generalized anxiety disorder.

Obsessive-Compulsive Disorder

Obsessions are recurrent, intrusive thoughts, impulses, or images that are perceived as inappropriate, grotesque, or forbidden. The obsessions, which elicit anxiety and marked distress, are termed "ego-alien" or "ego-dystonic" because their content is quite unlike the thoughts that the person usually has. Obsessions are perceived as uncontrollable, and the sufferer often fears that he or she will lose control and act upon such thoughts or impulses. Common themes include contamination with germs or body fluids, doubts (i.e., the worry that something important has been overlooked or that the sufferer has unknowingly inflicted harm on someone), order or symmetry, or loss of control of violent or sexual impulses.

Compulsions are repetitive behaviors or mental acts that reduce the anxiety that accompanies an obsession or "prevent" some dreaded event from happening. Compulsions include both overt behaviors, such as hand washing or checking, and mental acts including counting or praying. Not uncommonly, compulsive rituals take up long periods of time, even hours, to complete. . . .

Obsessive-compulsive disorder typically begins in adolescence to young adult life (males) or in young adult life (females). For most, the course is fluctuating and, like generalized anxiety disorder, symptom exacerbations [worsening of symptoms] are usually associated with life stress. Common comorbidities include major depressive disorder and other anxiety disorders. Approximately 20 to 30 percent of people in clinical samples with obsessive-compulsive disorder report a past history of tics, and about one-quarter of these people meet the full criteria for Tourette's disorder. Conversely, up to 50 percent of people with Tourette's disorder develop obsessive-compulsive disorder.

Obsessive-compulsive disorder has a clear familial pattern and somewhat greater familial specificity than most other anxiety disorders. Furthermore, there is an increased risk of obsessive-compulsive disorder among first-degree relatives with Tourette's disorder. Other mental disorders that may fall within the spectrum of obsessive-compulsive disorder include trichotillomania (compulsive hair pulling), compulsive shoplifting, gambling, and sexual behavior disorders. The latter conditions are somewhat discrepant because the compulsive behaviors are less ritualistic and yield some outcomes that are pleasurable or gratifying. Body dysmorphic disorder is a more circumscribed [limited] condition in which the compulsive and obsessive behavior centers around a preoccupation with one's appearance (i.e., the syndrome of imagined ugliness).

Acute and Post-Traumatic Stress Disorders

Acute stress disorder refers to the anxiety and behavioral disturbances that develop within the first month after exposure to an extreme trauma. Generally, the symptoms of an acute stress disorder begin during or shortly following the trauma. Such extreme traumatic events include rape or other severe physical assault, near-death experiences in accidents, witnessing a murder, and combat. The symptom of dissociation, which reflects a perceived detachment of the mind from the emotional state or even the body, is a critical feature. Dissociation also is characterized by a sense of the world as a dreamlike or unreal place and may be accompanied by poor memory of the specific events, which in severe form is known as dissociative amnesia. Other features of an acute stress disorder include symptoms of generalized anxiety and hyperarousal, avoidance of situations or stimuli that elicit memories of the trauma, and persistent, intrusive recollections of the event via flashbacks, dreams, or recurrent thoughts or visual images.

If the symptoms and behavioral disturbances of the acute stress disorder persist for more than 1 month, and if these features are associated with functional impairment or significant distress to the sufferer, the diagnosis is changed to post-traumatic stress disorder. Post-traumatic stress disorder is further defined . . . as having three subforms: acute (less than 3 months' duration), chronic

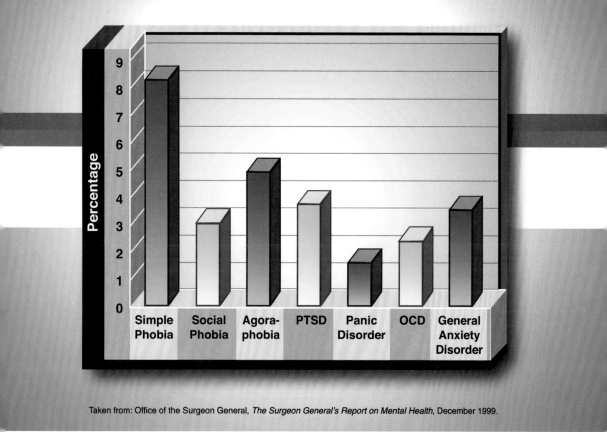

Prevalence of Anxiety Disorders

Taken from: Office of the Surgeon General, *The Surgeon General's Report on Mental Health*, December 1999.

(greater than 3 months' duration), and delayed onset (symptoms began at least 6 months after exposure to the trauma).

By virtue of the more sustained nature of post-traumatic stress disorder (relative to acute stress disorder), a number of changes, including decreased self-esteem, loss of sustained beliefs about people or society, hopelessness, a sense of being permanently damaged, and difficulties in previously established relationships, are typically observed. Substance abuse often develops, especially involving alcohol, marijuana, and sedative-hypnotic drugs.

About 50 percent of cases of post-traumatic stress disorder remit within 6 months. For the remainder, the disorder typically persists for years and can dominate the sufferer's life. A longitudinal study of Vietnam veterans, for example, found 15 percent of veterans to be suffering from post-traumatic stress disorder 19 years after combat exposure. In the general population, the 1-year prevalence is about 3.6 percent, with women having almost twice the prevalence of men. The highest rates of post-traumatic stress disorder are found among women who are victims of crime, especially rape, as well as among torture and concentration camp survivors. Overall, among those exposed to extreme trauma, about 9 percent develop post-traumatic stress disorder.

TWO

Many Teens Suffer from Anxiety Disorders

Sue Scheff

> Sue Scheff is the founder of Parents Universal Resource Experts, Inc. (PURE). PURE provides resources and information to help parents with the challenges of raising teenagers. Scheff is also the author of a book on raising teenagers and a frequent blogger on parenting teens and tweens. In this article Scheff explains how anxiety affects teens today. She discusses the symptoms, causes, and dangers of this prevalent condition. She also presents resources and suggestions to cope with and treat anxiety and warns that self-medication can lead to further problems.

The lesser known relative of depression, anxiety, afflicts people of all ages and can be especially detrimental for teenagers. It is completely normal and even common for individuals to experience anxiety, particularly during stressful periods, such as before a test or important date (think Prom). For many, this is beneficial, serving as motivation to study hard and perform well; however, for many, anxiety goes beyond standard high-stress periods. While occasional stress is nothing to worry about and can even be healthy, many people experience anxiety on an ongoing basis. People, especially teenagers, who suffer from anxiety disorders, find that their daily life can be interrupted by the intense, often long-lasting fear or worry.

Sue Scheff, "Teen Anxiety," Sue Scheff—Depression and Your Teen, March 4, 2009. www.sue scheff.org/sue-scheff-anxiety.html.

Anxiety disorders can cause headaches, stomachaches, loss of appetite, lack of concentration, and vomiting.

Anxiety disorders are not fatal; however, they can severely interfere with an individual's ability to function normally on a daily basis. The intense feelings of fear and worry often lead to a lack of sleep as it makes it very difficult for people to fall asleep. Those with anxiety disorders also commonly suffer from physical manifestations of the anxiety. The anxiety can cause headaches, stomach aches, and even vomiting. In addition stress can cause individuals to lose their appetite or have trouble eating. One of the more difficult aspects for students to deal with is difficulty concentrating. When one is consumed with worry, his or her mind continuously considers the worrisome thoughts, making it considerably harder for teenagers to concentrate on school work and other mentally intensive tasks. These effects of anxiety can make it difficult for teenagers to simply get through the day, let alone enjoy life and relax.

While there seems to be no single cause of anxiety disorders, it is clear that they can run in a family. The fact that anxiety disorders can run in families indicates that there may be a genetic or hereditary connection. Because a family member may suffer from an anxiety disorder does not necessarily mean that you will. However, individuals who have family members with this disorder are far more likely to develop it.

A Variety of Treatments

Within the brain, neurotransmitters help to regulate mood, so an imbalance in the level of specific neurotransmitters can cause a change in mood. It is this imbalance in a neurotransmitter called serotonin that leads to anxiety. Interestingly, an imbalance of serotonin in the brain is directly related to depression. For this reason, SSRI [selective serotonin reuptake inhibitor] medications more commonly referred to as anti-depressants, are often used to help treat an anxiety disorder. Medication can provide significant relief for those suffering from anxiety disorders; however, it is often not the most efficient form of treatment.

In addition to medication, treatments for anxiety disorders include cognitive-behavioral therapy, other types of talk therapy, and relaxation and biofeedback to control muscle tension. Talk therapy can be the most effective treatment for teenagers, as they discuss their feelings and issues with a mental health professional. Many teens find it incredibly helpful to simply talk about the stress and anxiety that they feel. Additionally, in a specific kind of talk therapy called cognitive-behavioral therapy teens actively "unlearn" some of their fear. This treatment teaches individuals a new way to approach fear and anxiety and how to deal with the feelings that they experience.

Self-Medication Is Dangerous

Many people attempt to medicate themselves when they suffer from stress or anxiety. While individuals find different ways to deal with the intense worry that they may experience, self medication can be very detrimental to their body. It is not uncommon

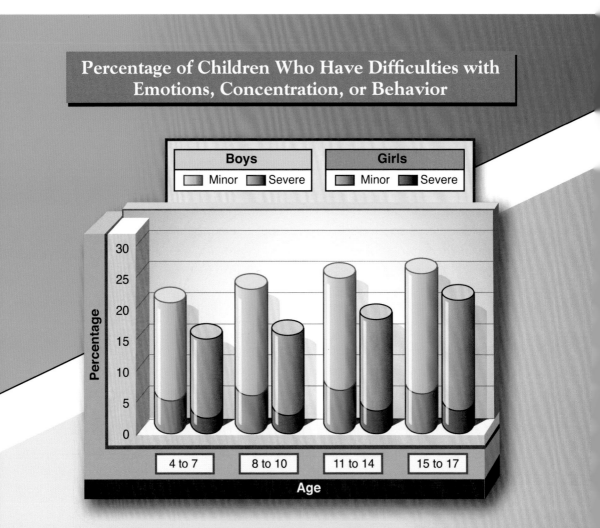

Taken from: Centers for Disease Control and Prevention, National Center for Health Statistics, 2006.

for people who suffer from anxiety disorders to turn to alcohol or drugs to relieve the anxiety. While this may provide a temporary fix for the afflicted, in the long run it is harmful. By relying on these methods, individuals do not learn how to deal with the anxiety naturally. Reliance on other substances can also lead to alcohol or drug abuse, which can be an especially significant problem if it is developed during the teen years.

Statistics on teen anxiety show that anxiety disorders are the most common form of mental disorders among adolescents: 8–10 percent of adolescents suffer from an anxiety disorder.

Symptoms of an anxiety disorder include: anger, depression, fatigue, extreme mood swings, substance abuse, secretive behavior, changes in sleeping and eating habits, bad hygiene or meticulous attention to it, compulsive or obsessive behavior.

One in eight adult Americans suffer from an anxiety disorder totaling 19 million people. Research conducted by the National Institute of Mental Health has shown that anxiety disorders are the number one mental health problem among American women and are second only to alcohol and drug abuse among men.

Anxiety disorders cost the U.S. $46.6 billion annually.

Anxiety sufferers see an average of five doctors before being successfully diagnosed.

THREE

Teens Should Receive Regular Mental Health Checkups

Peggy O'Farrell

Peggy O'Farrell is a staff writer for the *Cincinnati Enquirer*, covering health news and issues. In this article O'Farrell reports that the emergency room (ER) may be an effective location to screen teenagers for anxiety and other mental health and behavioral problems. Teens are reluctant to seek help for such issues but are often in the ER for other medical problems or injuries. ER personnel report success using Teen Screen, a questionnaire aimed at identifying mental health issues. According to the author, if Teen Screen—or a similar procedure— were adopted at more hospitals, doctors could detect the warning signs of mental illness and intervene before the conditions lead to more serious consequences.

Jacqueline Grupp-Phelan figured she'd spend her days in the emergency room [ER] treating kids for stomach flu, asthma attacks and broken bones.

She deals with all of those things. But Grupp-Phelan, an emergency medicine specialist at Cincinnati Children's Hospital Medical Center, also spends a lot of time trying to figure out if a teen's stomach ache or headache might mask serious depression or suicidal impulses.

Peggy O'Farrell, "Mental Health Checkups Urged for Teens," *Cincinnati Enquirer*, March 17, 2009. Reproduced by permission.

A recent screening of patients coming into the Cincinnati Children's ER for routine care found that about 70 percent had a significant mental health or behavioral problem, including depression, anxiety and social phobias, Grupp-Phelan said. About 40 percent had symptoms severe enough to interfere with patients' daily activities. "Their symptoms were impairing the things these kids are supposed to do, to go to school every day and do a good job and socialize with their friends," she said.

[In March 2009] Grupp-Phelan and other pediatricians from around the U.S. [talked] to Congressional leaders in Washington about mental health issues affecting youth. Their message is that pediatricians should adopt mental health checkups as part of their routine care for teenagers. "We've got lots of resources

Emergency room personnel report success in using the Teen Screen questionnaire, which is designed to identify mental health issues in teens.

in Cincinnati to help these kids, but first you've got to identify them," Grupp-Phelan said.

Depression and other mental illness play a role in physical illness, she said, but they're mostly linked to suicide and suicide attempts.

Doctors Can Help Spot Warning Signs

Parents and pediatricians need to do a better job of spotting the warning signs of depression and other mental illnesses that might contribute to suicidal behavior, Grupp-Phelan said.

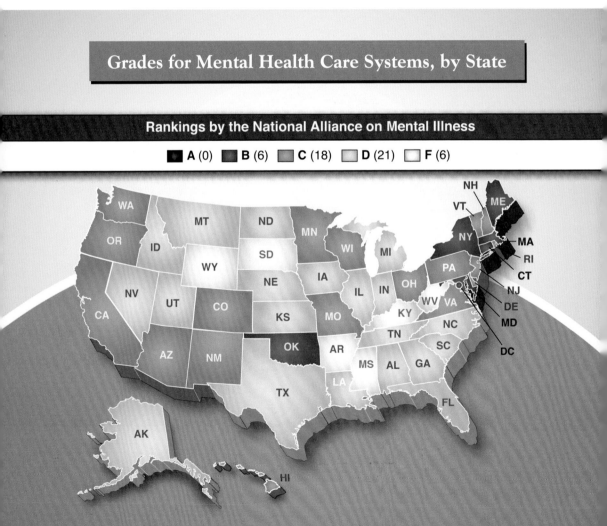

Grades for Mental Health Care Systems, by State

Rankings by the National Alliance on Mental Illness

A (0)   B (6)   C (18)   D (21)   F (6)

Taken from: National Alliance on Mental Illness. www.nami.org.

She and her colleagues at Cincinnati Children's have recently begun using Teen Screen, a brief questionnaire aimed at identifying mental health issues, for every teen who comes into the ER. "These kids don't see their pediatrician every year, but they do come in and see me when they've got a sore throat or a rash or a bad cold," she said. "We have to take advantage of those visits. These kids are in the ER for a long time. You might as well screen them while they're hanging out."

Teens' mental health issues are an area of growing concern for many pediatricians, said Chris Cunha, a Crestview Hills pediatrician. "We have more concerns year over year over year about the number of adolescents we're seeing with mood disorders," Cunha said. "I can see us moving very easily toward a routine screening mechanism."

Teens won't often volunteer information about their mood, said Jeffrey Drasnin, a pediatrician with offices in Milford and Hyde Park, but they'll answer questions—if the pediatrician can speak to them privately, away from their parents, for a few minutes. "It's a finite number of things you have to look for," he said. "Changes in friends or giving up activities, sleeping more or not sleeping at all. I ask, what do you do outside school? If they tell me, 'Oh, nothing; I just sit around,' then I ask, well, what did you used to do?"

Routine screening can held save lives, Grupp-Phelan said, and it can also help save money. "It's very expensive to take care of these kids in the emergency room," she said. "They come in with abdominal pains and they get significant workups, and radiological exposures and blood tests, and it's really for issues that aren't related to a physical problem."

FOUR

Managing Test Anxiety

Anxiety Disorders Association of America

> The Anxiety Disorders Association of America (ADAA) is the only national nonprofit organization solely dedicated to informing the public, health care professionals, and media that anxiety disorders are real, serious, and treatable. ADAA promotes the early diagnosis, treatment, and cure of anxiety disorders, and it is committed to improving the lives of the people who suffer from them. This viewpoint discusses the causes and symptoms of test anxiety, arguing that it can affect students' ability to learn and study effectively. The association also provides numerous strategies for avoiding or minimizing test anxiety.

You went to class, completed your homework, tackled tough essays and studied. You arrive at your exam confident you know the material. As you take your seat, you start to feel butterflies in your stomach and your palms begin to sweat.

Prepared for the test, your butterflies turn to nausea. You are sweating profusely. You feel lightheaded. Your heart is racing. Your mind is a blank. You want to run out of the room. You may have test anxiety. Read on for causes, symptoms and ways to manage test anxiety.

Anxiety Disorders Association of America, "Test Anxiety." www.adaa.org. Reproduced by permission.

What Is Test Anxiety?

Test anxiety is a type of performance anxiety—just like when some people get nervous speaking to large crowds or trying something new. Test anxiety occurs for a number of reasons.

Fear of failure. While the pressure to perform can act as a motivator, it can also be devastating to individuals who tie their self-worth to the outcome of a test.

Test anxiety can occur due to such things as lack of preparation, fear of failure, and a history of performing poorly on tests.

Lack of preparation. Waiting until the last minute or not studying at all can leave individuals feeling anxious and overwhelmed.

Poor test history. Previous problems or bad experiences with test-taking can lead to a negative mindset and influence performance on future tests.

What Are the Symptoms of Test Anxiety?

Individuals suffering from test anxiety may experience a variety of symptoms. These include:

Physical symptoms. Headache, nausea, diarrhea, excessive sweating, shortness of breath, rapid heartbeat, light-headedness and feeling faint can all occur. Test anxiety can lead to a panic attack, which is the abrupt onset of intense fear or discomfort in which individuals may feel like they are unable to breathe or having a heart attack.

Emotional symptoms. Feelings of anger, fear, helplessness and disappointment are common emotional responses to test anxiety.

Behavioral/cognitive symptoms. Difficulty concentrating, thinking negatively and comparing yourself to others are common symptoms of test anxiety.

How Can You Manage Your Test Anxiety?

Test anxiety can be so severe that it may interfere with your ability to learn, concentrate and study effectively. This may prevent you from performing well. The following tips may help you manage your test anxiety.

Be prepared. Develop good study habits. Study at least a week or two before the exam, in smaller increments of time and over a few days (instead of pulling an "all-nighter"). Try to simulate exam conditions by working through a practice test, following the same time constraints.

Develop good test-taking skills. Read the directions carefully, answer questions you know first and then return to the more difficult ones. Outline essays before you begin to write.

Maintain a positive attitude. Remember that your self-worth should not be dependent on or defined by a test grade. Creating

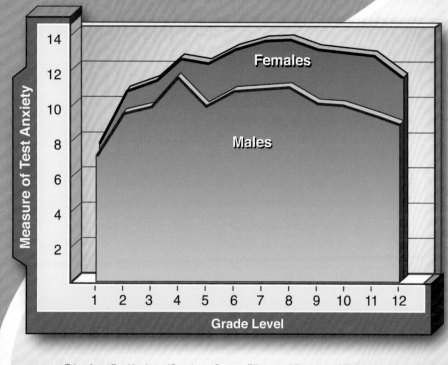

Average Test Anxiety Levels for Grades 1–12, Using the Test Anxiety Scale for Children (TASC)

Taken from: Ray Hembree, "Correlates, Causes, Effects, and Treatment of Test Anxiety," *Review of Educational Research*, vol. 58, no. 1, Spring 1988, pp. 44–77.

a system of rewards and reasonable expectations for studying can help to produce effective studying habits. There is no benefit to negative thinking.

Stay focused. Concentrate on the test, not other students during your exams. Try not to talk to other students about the subject material before taking an exam.

Practice relaxation techniques. If you feel stressed during the exam, take deep, slow breaths and consciously relax your muscles, one at a time. This can invigorate your body and will allow you to better focus on the exam.

Stay healthy. Get enough sleep, eat healthy, exercise and allow for personal time. If you are exhausted—physically or emotionally—it will be more difficult for you to handle stress and anxiety.

Visit the campus student services or counseling center. Schools are aware of the toll exams can take on students. They have offices/programs specifically dedicated to helping you and providing additional educational support so that you can be successful.

If these do not help you or you want additional help, talk to your doctor and find a local therapist.

How Can You Beat Anxiety Year-Round?

Do your best instead of trying to be perfect. We all know perfection isn't possible, so be proud of however close you get.

Take a time out. When you feel completely overwhelmed, take a deep breath and count to ten. Stepping back from the problem lets you clear your head. Do yoga. Meditate. Get a massage. Learn relaxation techniques. Listen to music.

Put things in perspective. Think about your situation. Ask yourself whether it's really as bad as you think it is or if you could be blowing it out of proportion.

Talk to someone. Don't let things bottle up to the verge of explosion. Reach out to your roommate, boyfriend, girlfriend or counselor if you're feeling low.

FIVE

Social Anxiety Disorder Is More than Just Shyness

Claudia Kalb

Claudia Kalb is a *Newsweek* general editor, focusing on health and medical issues. She has worked on a variety of cover stories, including features on alternatives to hormone therapy, prescription drug addiction, treatment for alcoholism, and Alzheimer's disease. In this article Kalb argues that social anxiety disorder is more than a bad case of shyness—it is a serious anxiety disorder that impacts peoples' lives. Yet this disorder frequently goes undiagnosed and untreated. Kalb discusses behavioral therapy techniques and medications that have shown promise.

It starts out just fine. You get invited to a party. You plan what you're going to wear, dream about whom you might meet. Then the big night arrives and, wham, the excitement sputters into nervousness. You stand around awkwardly, nurse a drink and ogle the chatty people around you. You feel shy.

You're not as alone as you think. Just about everyone is timid at some point, and plenty of people—almost half the population—qualify as shy most of the time. But what if every human encounter made you blush, tremble or perspire? What if your mind whirred incessantly with self-doubt ("I'm so stupid,"

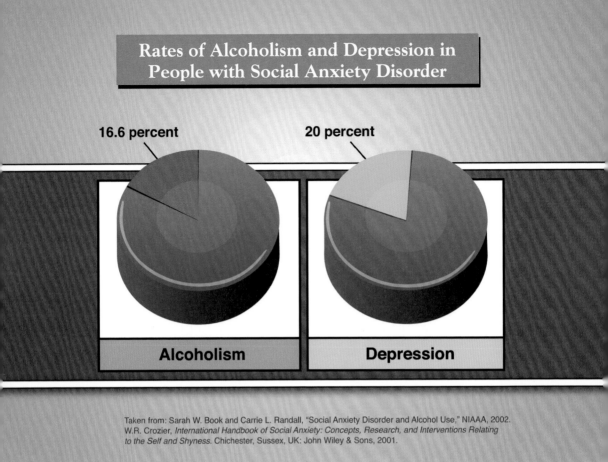

Rates of Alcoholism and Depression in People with Social Anxiety Disorder

16.6 percent

20 percent

Alcoholism

Depression

Taken from: Sarah W. Book and Carrie L. Randall, "Social Anxiety Disorder and Alcohol Use," NIAAA, 2002. W.R. Crozier, *International Handbook of Social Anxiety: Concepts, Research, and Interventions Relating to the Self and Shyness*. Chichester, Sussex, UK: John Wiley & Sons, 2001.

"I sound like a moron")? What if an obsession about what others were thinking kept you from keeping a job, even getting married? You may be suffering from social anxiety disorder, a diagnosable mental-health condition.

A Serious but Little-Known Problem

Most Americans, and even many doctors, have never heard of social anxiety disorder, yet it affects more than 5 million Americans, according to the National Institute of Mental Health. Drug companies, eager to expand their markets, are now spotlighting the disorder—and advertising medications to treat it. This spring [in 2003], Miami Dolphins running back Ricky Williams, diagnosed in 2001 and treated with the anti-depressant Paxil, kicked off a nationwide awareness campaign, funded by manufacturer GlaxoSmithKline. In the quick-fix society we live in, it's hard not to be skeptical: is inhibition a certifiable psychological problem? For clinicians who treat the problem, the answer is yes. "We see people whose lives have been trashed because of social anxiety disorder," says Richard Heimberg, head of the Adult Anxiety Clinic at Philadelphia's Temple University. "It's a horrid part of their existence."

Social anxiety disorder is more than just a bad case of shyness, intense and unremitting, it can make people feel worthless and powerless to move forward in their lives. Like almost every other human condition, the disorder appears to be triggered by a complex mix of genes (it runs in families) and environment, which could include growing up with anxious parents or relentless teasing by classmates—no one knows for sure. Technology is now helping to pinpoint changes in socially anxious brains. Using MRI [magnetic resonance imaging] scans, Dr. Murray Stein, of the University of California, San Diego, found that when people with the disorder are shown pictures of angry faces, their amygdala—the brain's fear center—lights up with more activity than it does in people without the condition. Now Stein is looking deeper to see if the amygdala itself is overreacting or if the problem starts even earlier in the processing of fear.

Brain circuitry matters little to Jonathan Wonnell, 34, who has spent much of his life avoiding social interaction. Quiet as a child, Wonnell isolated himself in high school—dating was out of the question. When his sisters threw a surprise birthday party for him, he froze in fear, incapable of enjoying the fun. "It was horrible," he says. Socializing still sets off a flurry of symptoms: his chest gets tight, he shifts his weight back and forth, he worries profoundly about being judged. "Inside, I'm just burning with anxiety," he says. Cognitive-behavioral therapy has been proved to help sufferers battle their demons—and it's helping Wonnell come out of his shell. In group meetings, participants speak in front of others, then talk about what they feared ("Everybody saw me blush") versus reality ("Nobody noticed"). Therapists ask patients to do homework in the real world, too, like asking someone out on a date. "People with social anxiety disorder have distorted thinking," says Jerilyn Ross, head of the Anxiety Disorders Association of America. "We're challenging their worst fears."

New Medications May Help

Medications are helping some patients as well. Earlier this year [in 2003], two antidepressants, Effexor and Zoloft, were approved for social anxiety disorder, joining Paxil, which hit the market in 1999. Other drugs, including Lexapro, may follow. Unlike therapy, though, relapse can be an issue once treatment stops. And the pills raise a critical question: could medicating social anxiety disorder lead to pathologizing [viewing as psychologically abnor-

Caused by a combination of genes and environment, social anxiety disorder can cause individuals to feel powerless, damaging their feelings of self-worth.

mal] normal shyness? "In an extroverted and drug-happy culture," says Wellesley College psychologist Jonathan Cheek, "the drugs are falling into fertile fields."

For now, though, specialists are more focused on getting help to those who need it. Social anxiety disorder, destructive on its own, can lead to depression and substance abuse. The key is to seek out and treat those who truly suffer—and let shy people enrich the world just as they are.

SIX

Obsessive-Compulsive Spectrum Disorders Are Linked to Brain Biology

Jeneen Interlandi

> Jeneen Interlandi is a health reporter for *Newsweek*. She reports that body dysmorphic disorder (BDD) is a legitimate anxiety disorder. Recent studies and research are dispelling the perception that BDD is "not a real condition." Like anorexia nervosa, BDD belongs to the group of disorders known as obsessive-compulsive spectrum disorders (OCSD). Studies show that the brains of people with BDD behave differently than those without the condition—they process images and respond to feedback differently. Such studies have helped health professionals better understand BDD, but much is still not known.

Aron Cowen spent most of his 20s in front of the mirror, despairing over his appearance. He used so much chemical straightener on his curly hair that it turned orange and started falling out. Two nose jobs only left him feeling worse about what he described as a crooked, bumpy profile. By the time the Los Angeles resident was 30, he had started measuring the lengths of his ears with a small ruler, convinced that one was bigger than the other. Still, he had a hard time convincing people that anything was wrong with him.

BDD Is a Serious Medical Condition

Even after a psychiatrist diagnosed Cowen with body dysmorphic disorder (BDD)—a rare psychiatric condition the sufferers of which see themselves as ugly and disfigured no matter how normal they look to others—family and friends remained certain that it was just "all in his head." Cowen says, "People tend to dismiss it as 'not a real condition.' They don't see the difference between me and any normal person who doesn't like some part of their appearance, so they just kind of want me to get over it."

A decade ago plenty of people, including many health professionals, would have agreed. Cowen's condition might have been written off by some as a desperate plea for attention, the result of

Body dysmorphic disorder is one of a family of disorders characterized by depression and obsessive thoughts that can render a person housebound and suicidal.

bad parenting, or perhaps a sign that Cowen himself was unable to cope with our appearance-obsessed society. In recent years, however, an increasing number of studies . . . have pointed the way to potential biological explanations for BDD and other behavioral disorders, such as anorexia nervosa. Doctors and patients can only hope that such tangible evidence of pathology will help remove the stigma attached to most mental illnesses.

BDD belongs to a family of disorders characterized by obsessive thoughts and repetitive behaviors that can render the worst of their victims housebound and suicidal. Known as Obsessive Compulsive Spectrum Disorders (OCSD), the group also includes anorexia, an eating disorder characterized by self-starvation, which has the highest mortality rate of any psychiatric illness. (The National Association of Anorexia Nervosa reports that 10 percent of anorexics die within a decade of developing the condition.) While BDD tends to affect men more often, and anorexia is more common among women, 30 percent of patients with one disorder also suffer from the other. Both conditions are rare: combined they affect less than 3 percent of the population.

Differences in Brain Function

In a paper published Monday [December 3, 2007] in the *Archives of General Psychiatry*, researchers at UCLA show that people suffering from BDD process visual images differently than healthy people. Study participants underwent a brain scan while viewing three different pictures of the same face: an untouched photo, a blurred photo and a finely detailed line drawing. While healthy subjects used the left, or more analytic, half of their brains only when processing the finely detailed images, subjects with BDD used their left brain to process all the images—suggesting that their minds were trying to extract minute details even where none existed. "This is the first demonstration of a potential biological contributor to BDD," says the study's lead author, James Feusner, medical director of UCLA's Obsessive Compulsive Disorder treatment program. "It tells us that there is an abnormality in how their brains interpret what they see."

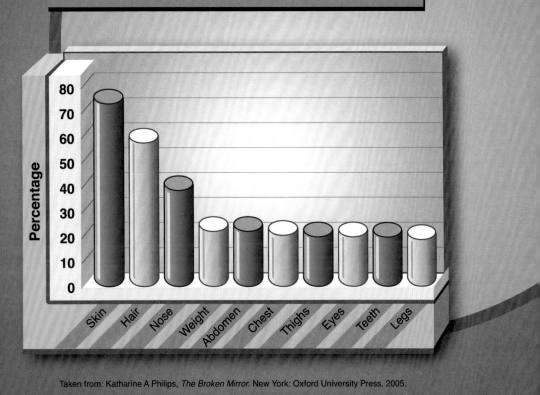

Ten Most Frequent Areas of Concern for Sufferers of Body Dysmorphic Disorder

Taken from: Katharine A Philips, *The Broken Mirror*. New York: Oxford University Press, 2005.

Using the same brain imaging technique, scientists at the University of Pittsburgh employed a guessing game to compare brain functioning in healthy women and in women who had once suffered from anorexia. In that study participants were asked to guess whether the next number to pop up on a screen would be higher or lower than five. Correct guesses were rewarded with $2, while incorrect guesses were penalized $1. In women who had never had anorexia, the anterior ventral striatum (AVS)—a brain region responsible for instant emotional responses—lit up each time they won. In former anorexics, however, the AVS was relatively unfazed by a win, indicating that the anorexic mind does not distinguish between positive and negative feedback.

What did light up in the anorexic brains, and what stayed lit throughout the guessing game, was the caudate region—a section of the brain involved in linking actions to outcomes and planning. "Healthy women were able to make a guess, feel a moment of delight or disappointment, and move on," explains the study's lead author, Walter Kaye, director of the eating disorder research program at the University of Pittsburgh Medical Center. "But women who had suffered from anorexia felt no thrill at winning and were plagued by a need to strategize and avoid guessing wrong." The findings mesh with some well-known characteristics of the eating disorder, which is most prevalent in white, affluent females. "Anorexics have trouble experiencing immediate pleasures and are typically preoccupied with a fear of making mistakes," says Kaye. "Now we can see that this cause-and-effect brain circuit is overactive and that the reward center is muted."

More Work to Be Done

Researchers have yet to determine whether faulty brain functioning causes OCSD or vice versa, and neither study manages to hint at new treatment strategies. Still, experts hope the findings may contribute something even more fundamental. "The thing that's been missing in psychiatry is the ability to relate behavioral disorders to some part of the brain that isn't working right," says Kaye. "We are learning more and more that conditions like anorexia are not willful acts meant to punish parents or get attention; they are serious medical conditions." With a little more hard evidence, he may just win over the skeptics.

SEVEN

Obsessive-Compulsive Disorder Can Be Treated

Psychology Today

> *Psychology Today* has a staff of writers, editors, and pro-
> grammers who have extensive expertise in the field of psy-
> chology, both from a clinical and an academic perspective.
> Many of its articles are written by, and rely upon informa-
> tion provided by, doctors and PhDs who have dedicated
> their professional lives to the promotion of sound psy-
> chology for the benefit of the communities in which they
> live. In the following article *Psychology Today* provides an
> overview of obsessive-compulsive disorder (OCD), dispel-
> ling previous misconceptions about the disease. OCD is
> more common than previously thought, as many suffer-
> ers go undiagnosed, and its causes are primarily biological,
> not environmental. The benefits of both behavioral and
> pharmacological treatments are discussed and compared.

Obsessive-compulsive disorder (OCD) is a potentially disabling
anxiety disorder. The person afflicted with OCD becomes
trapped in a pattern of repetitive senseless thoughts and behaviors
that are very difficult to overcome. A person's level of OCD can
be anywhere from mild to severe, but if severe and left untreated,
it can destroy a person's capacity to function at work, at school or
even to lead a comfortable existence in the home.

Obsessive-Compulsive Disorder Is Fairly Common

For many years, mental health professionals thought of OCD as a rare disease because only a small minority of their patients admitted to having the condition. The disorder often went unrecognized because many of those afflicted with OCD, ashamed of their repetitive thoughts and behaviors, failed to seek treatment. This led to underestimates of the number of people with the illness. However, a survey conducted in the early 1980s by the National Institute of Mental Health (NIMH) provided new knowledge about the prevalence of OCD. The NIMH survey showed that OCD affects more than 2 percent of the population, meaning that OCD is more common than such severe mental illnesses as schizophrenia, bipolar disorder or panic disorder. OCD strikes people of all ethnic groups. Males and females are equally affected.

Although OCD symptoms typically begin during the teen years or early adulthood, research shows that some children may even develop the illness during preschool. Studies indicate that at least one-third of cases of adult OCD began in childhood. Suffering from OCD during early stages of a child's development can cause severe problems for the child. It is important that the child receive evaluation and treatment as soon as possible to prevent the child from missing important opportunities because of this disorder.

Symptoms of Obsessive-Compulsive Disorder

Unwanted repetitive ideas or impulses frequently well up in the mind of the person with OCD. Persistent paranoid fears, an unreasonable concern with becoming contaminated or an excessive need to do things perfectly, are common. Again and again, the individual experiences a disturbing thought, such as, "This bowl is not clean enough. I must keep washing it." "I may have left the door unlocked." Or "I know I forgot to put a stamp on that letter." These thoughts are intrusive, unpleasant and produce a high degree of anxiety.

In response to their obsessions, most people with OCD resort to repetitive behaviors called compulsions. The most common of these are checking and washing. Other compulsive behaviors include repeating, hoarding, rearranging, counting (often while performing another compulsive action such as lock-checking). Mentally repeating phrases, checking or list making are also common. These behaviors generally are intended to ward off harm to the person with OCD or others. Some people with OCD have regimented rituals: Performing things the same way each time may give the person with OCD some relief from anxiety, but it is only temporary.

People with OCD show a range of insight into the uselessness of their obsessions. They can sometimes recognize that their obsessions and compulsions are unrealistic. At other times they may be unsure about their fears or even believe strongly in their validity.

Most people with OCD struggle to banish their unwanted thoughts and compulsive behaviors. Many are able to keep their obsessive-compulsive symptoms under control during the hours when they are engaged at school or work. But over time, resistance may weaken, and when this happens, OCD may become so severe that time-consuming rituals take over the sufferers' lives and make it impossible for them to have lives outside the home.

OCD tends to last for years, even decades. The symptoms may become less severe from time to time, and there may be long intervals when the symptoms are mild, but for most individuals with OCD, the symptoms are chronic.

Causes of Obsessive-Compulsive Disorder

The old belief that OCD was the result of life experiences has become less valid with the growing focus on biological factors. The fact that OCD patients respond well to specific medications that affect the neurotransmitter serotonin suggests the disorder has a neurobiological basis. For that reason, OCD is no longer attributed only to attitudes a patient learned in childhood—inordinate emphasis on cleanliness, or a belief that certain thoughts are dangerous or unacceptable. The search for causes now focuses on the interaction of neurobiological factors and environmental influences, as well as cognitive processes.

OCD is sometimes accompanied by depression, eating disorders, substance abuse, a personality disorder, attention deficit disorder or another of the anxiety disorders. Coexisting disorders can make OCD more difficult both to diagnose and to treat. Symptoms of OCD are seen in association with some other neurological disorders. There is an increased rate of OCD in people with Tourette's syndrome, an illness characterized by involuntary movements and vocalizations. Investigators are currently studying the hypothesis that a genetic relationship exists between OCD and the tic disorders.

Other illnesses that may be linked to OCD are trichotillomania (the repeated urge to pull out scalp hair, eyelashes, eyebrows or other body hair), body dysmorphic disorder (excessive preoccupation with imaginary or exaggerated defects in appearance) and hypochondriasis (the fear of having—despite medical evaluation and reassurance—a serious disease). Researchers are investigating the place of OCD within a spectrum of disorders that may share certain biological or psychological bases. It is currently unknown how closely related OCD is to other disorders such as trichotillomainia, body dysmorphic disorder and hypochondriasis.

There are also theories about OCD linking it to the interaction between behavior and the environment, which are not incompatible with biological explanations.

A person with OCD has obsessive and compulsive behaviors that are extreme enough to interfere with everyday life. People with OCD should not be confused with a much larger group of people sometimes called "compulsive" for being perfectionists and highly organized. This type of "compulsiveness" often serves a valuable purpose, contributing to a person's self-esteem and success on the job. In that respect, it differs from the life-wrecking obsessions and rituals of the person with OCD.

Treatments for Obsessive-Compulsive Disorder

Clinical and animal research sponsored by NIMH and other scientific organizations has provided information leading to both pharmacological and behavioral treatments that can benefit the person with OCD. One patient may benefit significantly from behavior

Prevalence of Alcohol, Tobacco, and Drug Use Among Individuals with Obsessive-Compulsive Disorder (OCD)

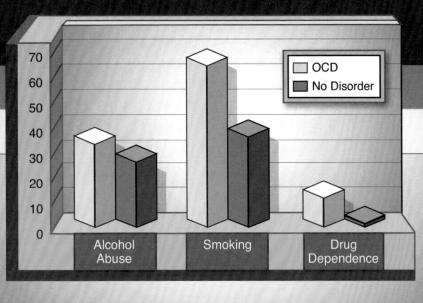

Taken from: Albina R. Torres, "Obsessive-Compulsive Disorder: Prevalence, Comorbidity, Impact, and Help-Seeking in the British National Psychiatric Morbidity Survey of 2000," *American Journal of Psychiatry*, November 2006.

therapy, yet another will benefit from pharmacotherapy. And others may benefit best from both. Others may begin with medication to gain control over their symptoms and then continue with behavior therapy. Which therapy to use should be decided by the individual patient in consultation with his or her therapist.

Clinical trials in recent years have shown that drugs that affect the neurotransmitter serotonin can significantly decrease the symptoms of OCD. The first of these serotonin re-uptake inhibitors (SRIs) specifically approved for the use in the treatment of OCD was the tricyclic anti-depressant clomipramine (Anafranil). It was followed by other SRIs that are called "selective serotonin re-uptake inhibitors" (SSRIs). Those that have been approved by the Food and Drug Administration for the treatment of OCD are fluoxetine (Prozac), fluvoxamine (Luvox) and paroxetine (Paxil). Another that has been studied in controlled clinical trials is sertraline (Zoloft).

Large studies have shown that more than three-quarters of patients are helped by these medications at least a little. And in more than half of patients, medications relieve symptoms of OCD by diminishing the frequency and intensity of the obsessions and compulsions. Improvement usually takes at least three weeks or longer. If a patient does not respond well to one of these medications, or has unacceptable side effects, another SRI may give a better response. For patients who are only partially responsive to these medications, research is being conducted on the use of an SRI as the primary medication and one of a variety of medications

One symptom of obsessive-compulsive disorder is a compulsion to perform repetitive behaviors such as washing the face or hands over and over.

as an additional drug (an augmenter). Medications are of help in controlling the symptoms of OCD, but often, if the medication is discontinued, relapse will follow.

Traditional psychotherapy, aimed at helping the patient develop insight into his or her problem, is generally not helpful for OCD. However, a specific behavior therapy approach called "exposure and response prevention" is effective for many people with OCD. In this approach, the patient deliberately and voluntarily confronts the feared object or idea, either directly or by imagination. At the same time the patient is strongly encouraged to refrain from ritualizing, with support and structure provided by the therapist, and possibly by others whom the patient recruits for assistance. For example, a compulsive hand washer may be encouraged to touch an object believed to be contaminated, and then urged to avoid washing for several hours until the anxiety provoked has greatly decreased. Treatment then proceeds on a step-by-step basis, guided by the patient's ability to tolerate the anxiety and control the rituals. As treatment progresses, most patients gradually experience less anxiety from the obsessive thoughts and are able to resist the compulsive urges.

Studies of behavior therapy for OCD find it to be a successful treatment for the majority of patients who complete it, and the positive effects endure once treatment has ended, if there are follow-up sessions and other relapse-prevention components. According to studies, [of] more than 300 OCD patients who were treated by exposure and response prevention, an average of 76 percent showed lasting results from 3 months to 6 years after treatment.

One study provides new evidence that cognitive-behavioral therapy may prove an effective aid for those with OCD. This variant of behavior therapy emphasizes changing the OCD sufferer's beliefs and thinking patterns. Further studies are required before cognitive-behavioral therapy can be adequately evaluated.

People with OCD will do best if they attend therapy, take all prescribed medications, seek support of family, friends, and a discussion group. When a family member suffers from obsessive-compulsive disorder it's helpful to be patient about their progress and acknowledge any successes, no matter how small.

EIGHT

A Debate Surrounds Veterans with Post-Traumatic Stress Disorder

Shankar Vedantam

Shankar Vedantam is a national correspondent writing about science and human behavior for *The Washington Post*. In addition to his articles, he writes a biweekly column titled "Department of Human Behavior." Here, Vedantam reports on the politically charged issue of treating veterans with post-traumatic stress disorder (PTSD). Recently, the number of veterans receiving disability payments for PTSD has spiked. This has triggered a debate, as some accuse the government of trying to limit these expensive payouts.

The spiraling cost of post-traumatic stress disorder [PTSD] among war veterans has triggered a politically charged debate and ignited fears that the government is trying to limit expensive benefits for emotionally scarred troops returning from Iraq and Afghanistan.

In the past five years [from 2000 to 2005], the number of veterans receiving compensation for the disorder commonly called PTSD has grown nearly seven times as fast as the number receiving benefits for disabilities in general, according to a report this year [2005] by the inspector general of the Department of Veterans Affairs [VA]. A total of 215,871 veterans received PTSD benefit payment last year at a cost of $4.3 billion, up from $1.7 billion in 1999—a jump of more than 150 percent.

Experts say the sharp increase does not begin to factor in the potential impact of the wars in Iraq and Afghanistan, because the increase is largely the result of Vietnam War vets seeking treatment decades after their combat experiences. Facing a budget crunch, experts within and outside the Veterans Affairs Department are raising concerns about fraudulent claims, wondering whether the structure of government benefits discourages healing, and even questioning the utility and objectivity of the diagnosis itself.

"On the one hand, it is good that people are reaching out for help," said Jeff Schrade, communications director for the Senate Veterans Affairs Committee. "At the same time, as more people reach out for help, it squeezes the budget further."

The PTSD Debate Becomes Political

Among the issues being discussed, he said, was whether veterans who show signs of recovery should continue to receive disability compensation: "Whether anyone has the political courage to cut them off—I don't know that Congress has that will, but we'll see."

Much of the debate is taking place out of public sight, including an internal VA meeting in Philadelphia this month [December 2005]. The department has also been in negotiations with the Institute of Medicine over a review of the "utility and objectiveness" of PTSD diagnostic criteria and the validity of screening techniques, a process that could have profound implications for returning soldiers.

The growing national debate over the Iraq war has changed the nature of the discussion over PTSD, some participants said. "It has become a pro-war-versus-antiwar issue," said one VA official who spoke on the condition of anonymity because politics is not supposed to enter the debate. "If we show that PTSD is prevalent and severe, that becomes one more little reason we should stop

The treatment of veterans for post-traumatic stress disorder has triggered a debate, largely out of public view, on whether the government is trying to limit expensive payouts to PTSD sufferers.

waging war. If, on the other hand, PTSD rates are low . . . that is convenient for the [president George W.] Bush administration."

As to whether budget issues and politics are playing a role in the agency's review of PTSD diagnosis and treatment, VA spokesman Scott Hogenson said: "The debate is over how to provide the best medical services possible for veterans."

PTSD Is Caused by Trauma

People with PTSD have paralyzing memories of traumatic episodes they experienced or witnessed, a range of emotional problems, and significant impairments in day-to-day functioning. Underlying the political and budget issues, many experts acknowledged, is a broader scientific debate over how best to diagnose trauma-related pathology, what the goal of treatment should be—even what constitutes trauma.

Harvard psychologist Richard J. McNally argues that the diagnosis equates sexual abuse, car accidents and concentration camps, when they are entirely different experiences: A PTSD diagnosis has become "a way of moral claims-making," he said. "To underscore the reprehensibility of the perpetrator, we say someone has been through a traumatic event."

Chris Frueh, director of the VA clinic in Charleston, S.C., said the department's disability system encourages some veterans to exaggerate symptoms and prolong problems in order to maintain eligibility for benefits. "We have young men and women coming back from Iraq who are having PTSD and getting the message that this is a disorder they can't be treated for, and they will have to be on disability for the rest of their lives," said Frueh, a professor of public psychiatry at the Medical University of South Carolina. "My concern about the policies is that they create perverse incentives to stay ill. It is very tough to get better when you are trying to demonstrate how ill you are."

Most veterans whom Frueh treats for PTSD are seeking disability compensation, he said. Veterans Affairs uses a sliding scale; veterans who are granted 100 percent disability status receive payments starting at around $2,300 a month. The VA inspector general's report found that benefit payments varied widely in states and said that was because VA centers in some states are more likely to grant veterans 100 percent disability.

Psychiatrist Sally Satel, who is affiliated with the conservative American Enterprise Institute, said an underground network advises veterans where to go for the best chance of being declared disabled. The institute organized a recent meeting to discuss PTSD among veterans.

Both Sides Question Diagnoses

Once veterans are declared disabled, they retain that status indefinitely, Frueh and Satel said. The system creates an adversarial relationship between doctors and patients, in which veterans sometimes take legal action if doctors decline to diagnose PTSD,

Frueh said. The clinician added that some patients who really need help never get it because they are unwilling to undergo the lengthy process of qualifying for disability benefits, which often requires them to repeatedly revisit the painful episodes they experienced.

The concern by Frueh and Satel about overdiagnosis and fraud—what researchers call "false positives"—has drawn the ire of veterans groups and many other mental health experts.

A far bigger problem is the many veterans who seek help but do not get it or who never seek help, a number of experts said. Studies have shown that large numbers of veterans with PTSD never seek treatment, possibly because of the stigma surrounding mental illness. "There are periodic false positives, but there are also a lot of false negatives out there," said Terence M. Keane, one of the nation's best-known PTSD researchers, who cited a 1988 study on the numbers of veterans who do not get treatment. "Less than one-fourth of people with combat-related PTSD have used VA-related services."

Larry Scott, who runs the clearinghouse http://www.vawatchdog .org/, said conservative groups are trying to cut VA disability programs by unfairly comparing them to welfare. Compensating people for disabilities is a cost of war, he said: "Veterans benefits are like workmen's comp. You went to war. You were injured. Either your body or your mind was injured, and that prevents you from doing certain duties and you are compensated for that."

Scott said Veterans Affairs' objectives were made clear in the department's request to the Institute of Medicine for a $1.3 million study to review how PTSD is diagnosed and treated. Among other things, the department asked the institute—a branch of the National Academies chartered by Congress to advise the government on science policy—to review the American Psychiatric Association's criteria for diagnosing PTSD. Effectively, Scott said, Veterans Affairs was trying to get one scientific organization to second-guess another.

PTSD experts summoned to Philadelphia for the two-day internal "expert panel" meeting were asked to discuss "evidence regarding validity, reliability, and feasibility" of the department's PTSD assessment and treatment practices, according to an e-mail

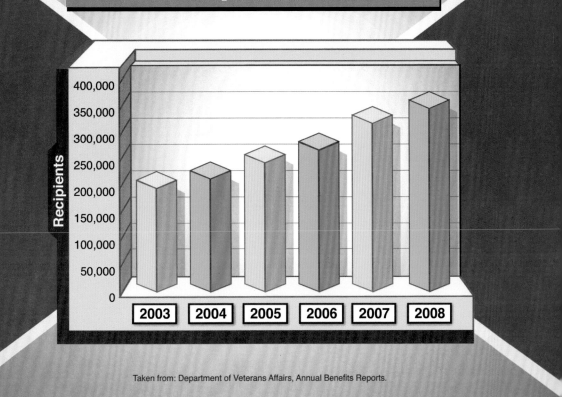

Number of Veterans Receiving Veterans Affairs Compensation for PTSD

Recipients

400,000
350,000
300,000
250,000
200,000
150,000
100,000
50,000
0

2003 2004 2005 2006 2007 2008

Taken from: Department of Veterans Affairs, Annual Benefits Reports.

invitation obtained by *The Washington Post*. The goal, the e-mail added, is "to improve clinical exams used to help determine benefit payments for veterans with Post Traumatic Stress Disorder."

"What they are trying to do is figure out a way not to diagnose vets with PTSD," said Steve Robinson, executive director of the National Gulf War Resource Center, a veterans advocacy group. "It's like telling a patient with cancer, 'if we tell you, you don't have cancer, then you won't suffer from cancer.'"

Hogenson, the VA spokesman, said the department is not seeking to overturn the established psychiatric criteria for diagnosing PTSD. "We are reviewing the utility and the objectivity of the criteria . . . and are commenting on the screening instruments used by VA," he said. "We want to make sure what we do for screening comports with the latest information out there."

NINE

Tranquilizers, Pills, and Shock Therapy Have Been Used to Treat Anxiety

Peggy Curran

Peggy Curran is the University Life reporter and columnist for *The Montreal Gazette*. In this viewpoint she examines a report on the history of anxiety in the United States and the use of tranquilizers to treat it. American culture has fostered anxiety, and Americans have been treating it with pills since the 1950s. The attitude toward medication has changed, but millions of Americans—encouraged by drug companies—are still taking anxiety medications.

"Every age says it is the most anxious," says Andrea Tone, Canada Research Chair in the social history of medicine at McGill University and the author of *The Age of Anxiety: A History of America's Turbulent Affair with Tranquilizers*, published this month [January 2009] by Basic Books. "You can't take history and flatten it out and compare the anxieties someone endured during the Crusades with a person struggling to feed their family during the Great Depression or a child today who has a phobia about helium balloons."

Tone's thoughtful, engaging book focuses on the development and phenomenal success of tranquilizers like Miltown, Valium and Librium during the 1950s and '60s. But she says demand for the next generation of tranquilizers like Xanax and Ativan has been "a growth industry" ever since the terrorist attacks on Sept. 11, 2001.

Anxiety Disorders Are on the Rise

In the weeks after the World Trade Centre bombing, sales of Xanax climbed by 22 per cent in New York and nine per cent across the United States. In the four years after the attacks, the number of Americans seeking help for anxiety rose from 13.4 million to 16.2 million. "Anxiety disorders are making a comeback," Tone said.

The election of Barack Obama as U.S. president is trumpeted by many as the dawn of an era of optimism and renewal, a human

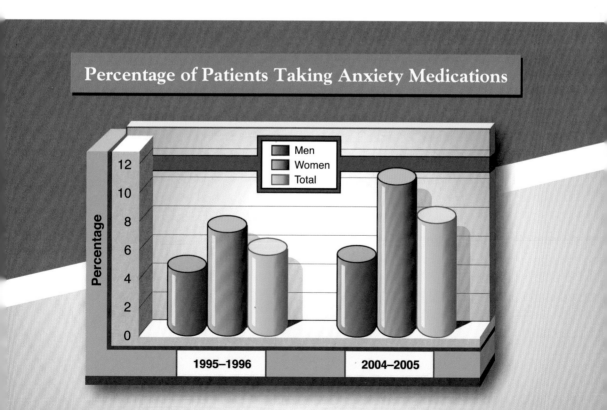

Taken from: National Center for Health Statistics, 2008.

antidote to the fear and loathing of recent months. But Tone is not persuaded the words or actions of any one person can quell the buzzing in the head and jittery feeling in the pit of the stomach of someone who is worried, phobic or overwrought. "There are lots of reasons for people to be anxious right now. There are financial concerns, people are losing their jobs. And of course, historically, prescriptions for anti-anxiety medication have always sold best in December and January, when all that spirit of family togetherness can be undermined by reality."

A 10-year study released by Statistics Canada found a strong link between low-income households and high psychological distress, with poverty, job losses, demotions or failure at school weighing more heavily on men and women from lower-income families than on affluent individuals.

Pills Have Been Popular for Decades

Nearly a decade ago, Tone was doing research for her previous book, an acclaimed history of contraceptives that was named one of the year's best books by the *Washington Post*, when she became fascinated with the other hugely popular pill that dominated the 1960s and '70s—the tranquilizers that revolutionized public attitudes toward anxiety disorders. In 1978 alone, manufacturers of Valium sold 2.3 billion tablets worldwide, "enough to medicate half the globe." Emotional aspirin, don't-give-a-damn pills, little peace pills, executive Excedrin and Mother's Little Helper.

From the mid-1950s through the late 1970s—right around the time former First Lady Betty Ford checked herself into rehab and a coroner's report revealed the late Elvis Presley had been guzzling vast doses of Valium and other prescription drugs—tranquilizers were seen as a great panacea [cure-all] for a society that, as television producer and self-professed pill-popper Barbara Gordon would later put it, was dancing as fast as it could.

"It is a tale of success and addiction, of pharmaceutical revolution and political revulsion, and of people's long-standing desire to appear calm on the outside when they feel frazzled within," said Tone.

A Little Anxiety Is Healthy

Of course, there's nothing wrong with a little tension, the butter-flies that push us to perform in a big exam or that frisson [shiver] of anxiousness psychologists refer to as the "fight-or-flight" response. "There is a threshold of anxiety which is healthy for us," said Tone. "If you are out hiking in the woods and meet up with a grizzly bear, you don't want to be so mellow that you say, 'Oh, look, a bear.' For a woman, walking alone late at night on an urban street, who sees a silhouette in the shadows, it's probably healthy to be a little anxious."

But when everyday stress gives way to phobias, until worries, fears and depression threaten the ability to cope or even get out of bed in the morning, intervention is required.

American Culture Encouraged Anxiety

Back in the late 19th-century, William James, pioneering American psychologist and brother of novelist Henry James, coined the term "Americanitis" for the angst—the official diagno-sis was neurasthenia—which afflicted people in all walks and sta-tions of life: shell-shocked Civil War veterans, women of wealth and privilege, even President Theodore Roosevelt. "The fast pace of life advanced the nation but depleted the energies of its most determined denizens," Tone writes. "In medical and cultural terms, neurasthenia in the late nineteenth and early twentieth centuries was regarded (much as anxiety would be in the 1950s) as the price Americans paid for their stunning success."

Early treatments for anxiety ranged from opium and electro-shock therapy to sponge baths, digitalis and the alcohol-fueled elixirs and nerve medicines sold by door-to-door peddlers. By the early 1950s, talk therapy was the standard prescription, although that didn't stop some people from resorting to a hazardous com-bination of "uppers" and "downers"—the amphetamines and bar-biturates that set the stage for Jacqueline Susann's cheesy classic novel *Valley of the Dolls*.

As a social historian, Tone was curious to see how the intro-duction of tranquilizers in 1955—and the enthusiastic embrace

Nineteenth-century American psychologist William James coined the term "Americanitis" to describe the angst so prevalent in American society.

they received—both reflected and changed social behaviour in the United States—the same can also be said for Canada, Britain and western Europe. "Anxiety was viewed less as a serious psychiatric disorder than as a badge of achievement: an emblem of struggle, but also of success. Anxiety was the predictable yet commendable offshoot of Americans' insatiable hunger to get ahead," she writes.

"We need to understand the decision to take a 'trank' [tranquilizer] as an individual act which, because it was made by millions of Americans, prompted widespread commentary and catalyzed long-lasting medical and political change." She argues "the rise of America's tranquilizer culture cannot be understood apart from the political and cultural events that shaped it." Among these, she said, were atomic anxiety in the Cold War era and "a convenience mentality that prized quick, easy, and cheap fixes for social and personal problems."

A Faith in Pills

But there was also an unchallenged, naive, almost patriotic, faith in pharmaceutical solutions in the wake of the discovery of penicillin and polio vaccines, new treatments for diabetes and hypertension. "This was before thalidomide, before the horrors of DES [both of which caused severe birth defects] and side effects from oral contraceptives popped the bubble of enthusiasm, prompting people to begin questioning the safety of medications and to do their own research," said Tone. "Big Pharma wasn't so big, but what it was doing was revolutionary."

Tone is anxious that her book not be seen as an indictment of the pharmaceutical industry. "My intention is not to demonize the pharmaceutical industry. I see this as a success story, while identifying the risks of over-diagnosis. It's not all good and not all bad."

One of the best discoveries Tone made during her research came during interviews with Frank Berger, a refugee from Hitler's Europe who invented Miltown by chance while looking for a longer-lasting version of penicillin. "You expect things to play out in a certain way," she said, recalling how she grew to like and respect Berger, who died last year [2008]. "He was a left-wing humanitarian troubled by the fact the United States still did not have universal health care." Throughout his career, he also refused to use salesmen to pitch Miltown to doctors in the years before advertising bans were eased. "He insisted salesmanship should not be confused with science."

Tone admits to having had her own close encounter with anti-anxiety medication briefly a few years ago after a turbulent post 9/11 flight left her temporarily spooked. "Most of us know someone—a mother, an uncle, a neighbor, perhaps even ourselves—who has taken Valium, Ativan, Miltown," Tone confesses in the book's preface. "Millions have, although they don't always admit it. I too chafed at the stigma, struggling with the implications of what it meant to need a tranquilizer to fly. But it worked. Several months later, I was back in the air. Soon, I was flying drug-free."

More Caution Today

Public attitudes toward medication as miraculous and benign began to shift in the early 1960s on the heels of the thalidomide disaster. The sedative, responsible for thousands of miscarriages and birth defects in Europe, had been kept off the American market, largely due to the vigilance of a newcomer to the Food and Drug Administration, the Canadian-born, McGill-trained, scientist Frances Oldham Kelsey.

Over the next decade, Tone suggests, the feminization of tranquilizer use also played a role in the increased stigmatization of anti-anxiety medication. In 1950s, Miltown was widely used, mostly by men. Drug abuse was seen as limited to people on the margins of society—returning veterans, the underclass, hippies. By the late 1970s, admissions by [people like] Betty Ford . . . made it clear the middle-classes were not immune, "that drugs were coming into the home, that Mom could be washing the kitchen floor and popping tranquilizers."

As neuroscientists became more aware of the physiological basis for a range of anxiety disorders, a new class of anti-depression medications upstaged tranquilizers—but did not replace them. Nowadays, Tone said, the person with everyday fears and worries, who needs the occasional hit to get to sleep or board a plane, is still more likely to find solace in tranquilizers than in anti-depressants like Paxil and Zoloft. They just don't talk about their neuroses as openly as their parents might have.

"Tranquilizers were fashionable, there was a chicness to them. There was a cachet to it that doesn't surround it now. We are more cynical now. Anxiety has been recast as a serious psychiatric disorder. It has taken on a medical gravitas which didn't exist in the 1950s, when there were drug-inspired cocktails like the Miltini and people like [comedians] Milton Berle and Jerry Lewis could make jokes at the Oscars about serving buttered Miltowns backstage to anyone who couldn't take the pressure."

TEN

Drug Companies Push Anxiety Treatments Unnecessarily

Linda Marsa

Linda Marsa is an award-winning Los Angeles–based investigative journalist, author, and teacher specializing in science, medicine, and health. Marsa is also the author of *Prescription for Profits: How the Pharmaceutical Industry Bankrolled the Unholy Marriage Between Science and Business*, about the corporate takeover of academic research and its disastrous impact on public health. In this article she argues that Americans are overmedicating. Drug companies' advertising campaigns have increased the demand for antianxiety pills, and people with normal levels of anxiety—not disorders—are getting prescriptions. The drug companies are profiting, says Marsa, but many people who do not need the pills suffer side effects without receiving benefits.

The ads seem to be everywhere, on TV, in magazines, doctors' offices, the Internet: Are you feeling tense? Having difficulty sleeping? Scared of criticism? If so, they suggest, the answer could be a pill—an antidepressant, to be exact.

The drugs that revolutionized the treatment of depression a decade ago now are increasingly used to treat anxiety disorders, mental illnesses that can cause paralyzing worry or intense fear of social situations. Caused by a deficiency in brain chemistry, the disorders can indeed be remedied by potent mood-altering medications such as Paxil and Effexor.

Drug companies commonly seek new uses for their drugs; it's a way of expanding their market and getting a greater return on the money spent doing research. But now it appears they could be capturing a new segment of patients—those with less serious disorders, such as occasional anxiety.

Since the federal government approved the drugs for generalized anxiety disorder and social phobia, prescriptions for the medications have soared. Doctors and other health experts, meanwhile, report a marked increase in the number of patients claiming anxiety disorders and seeking relief.

Medications May Be Overused

Just about everyone has experienced situational anxieties—when personal or professional stress keeps us keyed up and disturbs our sleep—and it can be difficult to pinpoint exactly when life's mundane worries escalate into a full-blown psychiatric disorder. "There are few conditions where there's a black and white cutoff," said Dr. Franklin Schneier, a psychiatrist at Columbia University in New York.

Consequently, some mental health experts say, people with normal angst may get powerful medications they don't need, sometimes suffering from side effects such as agitation, insomnia, loss of libido and, when they try to quit the drugs, withdrawal. At a time when managed-care companies are cutting expenses, this marketing of the drugs also ratchets up consumer demand for costly, name brands when generics, or even counseling, may do the job just as well.

Doctors and psychologists say the broad push to prescribe medications for anxiety is further indication we're medicalizing normal variations in temperament. The advertising is "a double-edged sword," said Dr. Michael Brase, medical director for behavioral services for WellPoint Health Networks Inc., the parent of Blue Cross of California. "It's helped some people realize they need to be on medication, but others may be just going though a bad patch in their lives. And that's what muddies the waters."

GlaxoSmithKline, the maker of Paxil, says the advertising campaigns de-stigmatize anxiety disorders in the same way that publicity surrounding the introduction of Prozac brought depression out of the closet 15 years ago. "Our intention is to educate the public about the symptoms of these disorders" so that people with serious mental illnesses will seek treatment, said Dr. Philip Perera, a psychiatrist and group director for clinical psychiatric research at GlaxoSmithKline in Philadelphia.

But it's the publicity that has caused many mental health experts to suspect that many people are getting medications for mental disorders that were once believed to be relatively rare. For example, after Paxil was approved to treat social pho-

Aggressive advertising of antidepressants such as Paxil by pharmaceutical companies has led to increased use of the drugs to treat people with normal levels of anxiety.

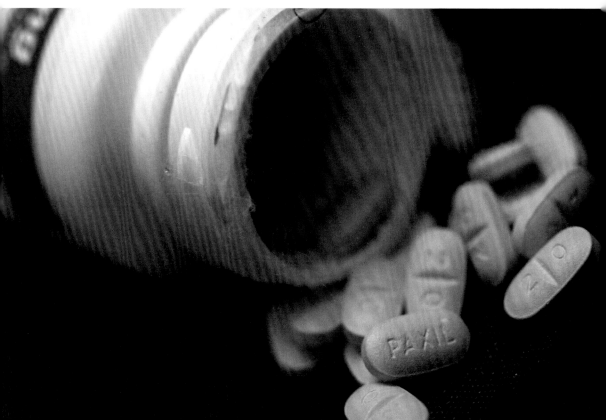

bia in 1999, the company nearly tripled its advertising spending, from $31.5 million in 1999 to $91.7 million in 2000. In April 2001, the FDA [Food and Drug Administration] approved the drug for generalized anxiety disorder as well. In the first six months of 2002, advertising for the drug topped the $60-million mark, according to figures compiled by CMR, a market research company.

The Pills May Help, but Companies Want Profit

Prescriptions are rising accordingly. Last year [2001] 26 million prescriptions for Paxil were dispensed. This year, more than 16.9 million prescriptions were filled in the first half of the year, a projected spike of more than 25%. Similarly, in 1999, when Effexor was approved to treat generalized anxiety, 5.5 million prescriptions were written for the drug; the following year, that figure rose to 8.7 million, according to IMS Health, a health-care information company in Fairfield, Conn.

"Advertising definitely induces demand for these products," said Steven Findlay, director of research for the National Institute for Health Care Management, a Washington, D.C., nonprofit. "But we don't know what percentage of these prescriptions are being written inappropriately."

Dan Kabic is one Paxil user who believes he shouldn't have been given the drug. The 31-year-old marketing manager from San Jose said he started taking Paxil two years ago when he was suffering from insomnia. His sleeping pills were no longer working and, he said, "my doctor thought anxiety was causing my sleeping problems."

But the medication made Kabic feel worse, he said. His weight plummeted, he lost interest in sex, he felt like a zombie—and he still couldn't sleep. "It really interfered with my life," said Kabic, who's been weaning himself off of Paxil.

One out of every five people will suffer from an anxiety disorder at some time, according to Ronald Kessler, a researcher at Harvard Medical School in Boston. Such disorders include obsessive-compulsive disorder, panic attacks, post-traumatic stress

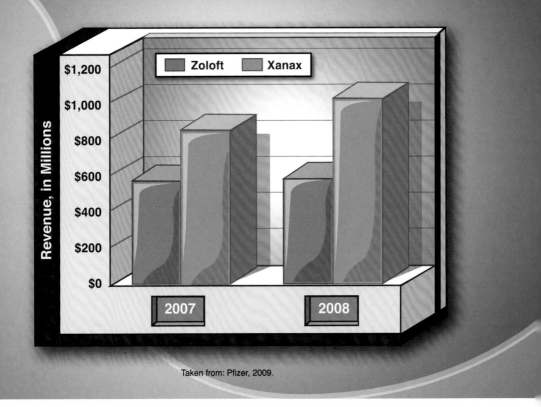

Product Revenues from Selected Antianxiety Medications

Revenue, in Millions

$1,200
$1,000
$800
$600
$400
$200
$0

Zoloft Xanax

2007 2008

Taken from: Pfizer, 2009.

syndrome and the two most common—social phobia and generalized anxiety.

Generalized anxiety disorder afflicts about 4% of the population, the 10 million worry warts who are paralyzed by irrational fears. Unlike people who are socially phobic, they don't fear human contact; they fret constantly about everything. "They're like 'worry machines,'" said Jerilyn Ross, president of the Anxiety Disorders Assn. of America in Silver Spring, Md. "They can't eat, they can't sleep, they're irritable and jumpy, and you can't calm them down with facts."

Similarly, anywhere from 3% to 13% of the population is crippled by social phobia, or social anxiety disorder, in which people are filled with intense dread and avoid everyday social situations.

Social phobics fear public humiliation or being judged by others, and may turn down a promotion, quit their jobs, or avoid leaving the house rather than deal with people. But the line between generalized anxiety disorder and normal fears is not as clear as it may seem. Almost half of all Americans—40% to 45%, according to recent polls—consider themselves shy, which is not a psychological disorder. Here again, it's tricky determining when shyness is debilitating enough to require pharmaceutical interventions.

"It's to the advantage of the drug companies to blur that line," said Bernardo J. Carducci, a professor of psychology and director of the Shyness Research Institute at Indiana University in New Albany. "All of a sudden, that gives them a tremendous market."

Doctors May Be Overprescribing

Family physicians dispense about 60% of the prescriptions for antidepressants, but they spend an average of only seven minutes with a patient, so there often isn't enough time to do an adequate psychological assessment, Brase said. Consequently, when patients insist they want a particular drug, doctors often cave in, rather than reviewing other therapeutic options.

"Patients come in with a perception that this medication is going to work for them, and if physicians take the time to challenge that assumption, there's often a credibility issue—almost like the patients don't believe them," said Martin Fornataro, the West Coast director of pharmacy for Cigna HealthCare in Glendale. "So physicians end up capitulating to their demands." On the other hand, some doctors must spend so much time clarifying whether a drug is warranted that the discussions can "crowd out more important things that need to be discussed," said Dr. Les Zendle, associate medical director for Kaiser Permanente Southern California in Pasadena.

Managed-care companies such as Kaiser Permanente and Cigna have begun educating physicians and patients about the pros and cons of direct-to-consumer advertising. And at Kaiser, patients are encouraged to seek counseling and learn better ways of managing stress. "Sometimes, people may just need some reassurance that their reactions are normal," Zendle said.

ELEVEN

An Illegal Drug Could Offer Legitimate Help to Anxiety Sufferers

Amy Turner

> Amy Turner has written articles published in *The Times* and *The Sunday Times*, major newspapers in the United Kingdom. She was nominated for Young Journalist of the Year for 2009 by the Press Gazette British Press Awards. In the following viewpoint Turner reports on the work of doctors who have found that the drug Ecstasy (MDMA) could be used to treat post-traumatic stress disorder. She details clinical trials in which it has shown promise. However, she notes that the illegal use of Ecstasy as a recreational designer drug raises concerns about legalizing it for treatment of post-traumatic stress disorder (PTSD). Despite Ecstasy's medical promise, the social and political hurdles may make it difficult for this treatment to catch on.

An Ecstasy tablet. That's what it took to make Donna Kilgore feel alive again—that and the doctor who prescribed it. As the pill began to take effect, she giggled for the first time in ages. She felt warm and fuzzy, as if she was floating. The anxiety melted away. Gradually, it all became clear: the guilt, the anger, the shame.

Before, she'd been frozen, unable to feel anything but fear for 10 years. Touching her own arms was, she says, "like touching a corpse." She was terrified, unable to respond to her loving husband or rock her baby to sleep. She couldn't drive over bridges for fear of dying, was by turns uncontrollably angry and paralyzed with numbness. When she spoke, she heard her voice as if it were miles away; her head felt detached from her body. "It was like living in a movie but watching myself through the camera lens," she says. "I wasn't real."

Unknowingly, Donna, now 39, had post-traumatic stress disorder (PTSD). And she would become the first subject in a pioneering American research program to test the effects of [methylenedioxymethamphetamine] (MDMA)—otherwise known as the dancefloor drug Ecstasy—on PTSD sufferers.

MDMA Could Help People Such as Donna

Some doctors believe MDMA could be the key to solving previously untreatable deep-rooted traumas. For a hard core of PTSD cases, no amount of antidepressants or psychotherapy can rid them of the horror of systematic abuse or a bad near-death experience, and the slightest reminder triggers vivid flashbacks.

PTSD-specific psychotherapy has always been based on the idea that the sufferer must be guided back to the pivotal moment of that trauma—the crash, the battlefield, the moment of rape—and relive it before they can move on and begin to heal. But what if that trauma is insurmountable? What if a person is so horrified by their experience that even to think of revisiting it can bring on hysterics? The Home Office estimates that 11,000 clubbers take Ecstasy every weekend. Could MDMA—the illegal class-A rave drug, found in the system of Leah Betts when she died in 1995, and over 200 others since—really help? Dr Michael Mithoefer, the psychiatrist from South Carolina who struggled for years to get funding and permission for the study, believes so. Some regard his study—approved by the US government—as irresponsible, dangerous even. But Mithoefer's results tell a different story. . . .

The author argues that war veterans suffering from PTSD should have the option of being treated with the illegal drug MDMA (Ecstasy).

A Traumatizing Experience

In 1993, Donna was brutally raped. . . . Afterwards, convinced that getting on with life was the best thing for herself and her child, Donna carried on as usual. . . . But she couldn't remember much of the attack itself, and didn't try. So she was surprised when, four years later, her symptoms started to kick in. "I had no idea it was PTSD. I couldn't understand why I was so angry, why I was having nightmares, flashbacks, fainting spells, migraine, why I felt so awful, like my body was stuffed with cotton wool. Things had been going so good."

She started drinking heavily and went from relationship to relationship, finding men hard to trust and get close to.

Convinced that she was dying and wouldn't live to see her next birthday, she went to the Air Force psychiatrist. "And that's where it started—take this pill, that pill. I've been on every kind of antidepressant—Zoloft, Celexa, Lexapro, Paxil. Wellbutrin made me feel suicidal. Prozac did the same. The pills were just masking the symptoms, I wasn't getting any better."

Yet she met her "soul mate," Steve, and married him in 2000. "When I first saw him I thought, 'This is the man I'm going to spend the rest of my life with.' We were like one person, finishing each other's sentences," she says. They muddled along, with Donna putting on a brave face. She had two more children. But getting close wasn't easy: "The longer we were married, the worse I got."

Once, Steve and Donna were watching TV when she had a vivid flashback to the night she was raped. "I looked at the door, I saw it open, and that feeling came over me all over again. I thought, 'My God, why won't this go away?' Steve tried to understand, but unless you've been through this, you don't know what it's like."

Donna moved to South Carolina in 2002 when Steve—also in the service—was posted there. She began seeing a psychiatrist called Dr Marcet, who diagnosed her with PTSD and attributed it to the rape. It helped to know that whatever it was had a name and a cause: "I was like, why hasn't anybody told me this before?" It was Marcet who referred her to the Mithoefers.

A New Treatment

Donna had never taken Ecstasy before. "I was a little afraid, but I was desperate. I had to have some kind of relief. I didn't want to live any more. This was no way to wake up every morning. So I met Dr Mithoefer. I said, 'Doctor, I will do anything short of a lobotomy. I need to get better.'" That's how, in March 2004, Donna became the first of Mithoefer's subjects in the MDMA study. Lying on a futon, with Mithoefer on one side of her and his wife, Annie, a psychiatric nurse, on the other, talking softly to her, she swallowed the small white pill. It was her last hope.

"After 5 or 10 minutes, I started giggling and I said, 'I don't think I got the placebo,'" she recalls. "It was a fuzzy, relaxing, on-a-different-plane feeling. Kind of floaty. It was an awakening." For the first time Donna faced her fears. "I saw myself standing on top of a mountain looking down. You know you've got to go down the mountain and up the other side to get better. But there's so much fog down there, you're afraid of going into it. You know what's down there and it's horrible.

"What MDMA did was clear the fog so I could see. Down there was guilt, anger, shame, fear. And it wasn't so bad. I thought, 'I can do this. This fear is not going to kill me.' I remembered the rape from start to finish—those memories I had repressed so deeply." Encouraged by the Mithoefers, Donna expressed her overwhelming love for her family, how she felt protected by their support and grateful for their love.

MDMA is well known for inducing these compassionate, "loved-up" feelings. For Donna, the experience was life-changing. So what happened when she went home? Was she cured? She sighs. "I don't know if there's such a thing as a cure. But after the first session I got up the next day and went outside, and it was like walking into a crayon box—everything was clear and bright. I did better in my job, in my marriage, with my kids. I had a feeling I'd never had before—hope. I felt I could live instead of exist."

How the Treatment Works

What makes MDMA so useful, Mithoefer believes, is the trust it establishes. "Many people with PTSD have a great deal of trouble trusting anybody, especially if they've been betrayed by someone who abused their trust, like a parent or a caregiver," he says. "MDMA has this effect of lowering fear and defences. It also allows more compassion for oneself and for others. People can revisit the trauma, feel the original feelings but not be retraumatized, not feel overwhelmed or have to numb out to cope with it." . . .

The patient lies on the futon in the Mithoefers' living-room-style office in Charleston, South Carolina. They wear eye shades to encourage introspection, and headphones through which relaxing music is played. Annie keeps an eye on the blood-pressure cuffs and temperature gauge. Mithoefer sits opposite, taking notes. Each patient is given a recording of their session afterwards.

The patient takes either a 125mg tablet of MDMA or a placebo pill, followed by a 62.5mg dose about two hours into the therapy session. The study is double-blind, so only the emergency nurse who carries the drugs from the safe to the office knows whether the patient is getting the drug. "We can always tell whether it's real or placebo. The patient can't—some people thought they got MDMA when they didn't," says Mithoefer. "But we're seeing very encouraging results. There's a real difference between placebo patients and patients who got MDMA, in terms of their ability to relive the trauma." . . .

At the time the Mithoefers treated Donna, in March 2004, their study had been a long time in the pipeline. Convinced of MDMA's potential, Rick Doblin, founder of the Multidisciplinary Association for Psychedelic Studies (Maps), had been in and out of the courts seeking permission from the Food & Drug Administration for clinical research since 1984. Maps, a group set up to fund psychedelic research, agreed to fund Mithoefer's study in 2000. The next year the FDA approved it. Then approval was withdrawn because of research by the neurologist George Ricuarte, at Johns Hopkins University, claiming that MDMA was lethally toxic. Even a single use, he reported, could cause brain damage and possibly Parkinson's disease. Ricaurte retracted his findings in 2002 when it turned out that bottles had been mixed up and the monkeys used as subjects had received lethal doses of methamphetamine (speed), rather than MDMA. "It was incredibly frustrating," Mithoefer says.

Mithoefer's study, which looks set to cost [$1 million] by the time it finishes in four years' time, is scrupulously monitored. Doblin had 1,000g of MDMA made specially, each gram costing $4. Mithoefer had to obtain a licence from the Drug Enforcement Administration (DEA), which keeps track of exactly how much MDMA each licence-holder has, and periodically checks the stocks for purity. A defibrillator must be kept in the building at all times in case of cardiac arrest, and an emergency nurse must be present during the treatment session. Once the study is complete, it will be subject to peer review. Then, all being well, Mithoefer hopes to see MDMA therapy available on prescription, administered in controlled surroundings, in 5 to 10 years. . . .

Potential Problems

But what about the potential for post-study abuse? Might someone who felt deflated after the elation of their MDMA session find the urge to self-medicate irresistible and pop to that 15-year-old on the corner for a quick fix? Not at all, says [Dr. Ben] Sessa. "I prescribe Valium all the time, and when the course is finished the patient could go and buy Valium on the street, but they don't. Very few people are interested in recreational drugs."

I ask Donna the same question. "Would I take the drug again? Yes, definitely," she says. "But not without a therapist. It's illegal."

Another former patient of Mithoefer's, a 42-year-old woman, had severe PTSD after being repeatedly and horrifically beaten and locked in a basement by her father during childhood. She wished to remain anonymous because she is still in contact with her parents. When I asked her the question, she replied: "I did it to get better, not to get high. Before the treatment, I would drink to hide my symptoms. But I don't want to get drunk now, let alone take drugs. I just don't need it any more."

The harmful effects of MDMA are still under investigation. The type of research that is carried out—normally with animals or with recreational users who also take other drugs—means that the exact levels of toxicity it causes are unknown. In 2006 Dr Maartje de Win of the University of Amsterdam published research showing that Ecstasy could cause depression, anxiety and long-term memory damage after one small dose. "We really don't know how much Ecstasy affects the brain in the long term," she says. "I would be very cautious about giving it therapeutically. We need to conduct much more research. And even then it should only be given as a last resort, after weighing the benefits against the risk of harm."

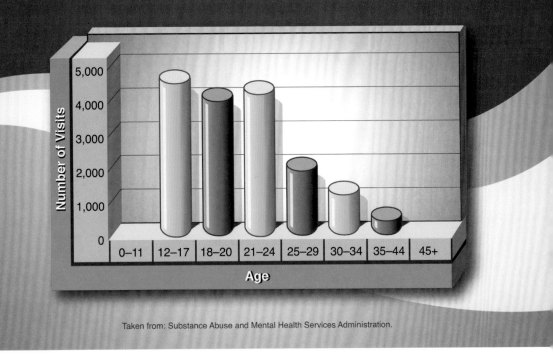

Ecstasy-Related Emergency Medical Visits in 2006, by Age

Taken from: Substance Abuse and Mental Health Services Administration.

Sessa is adamant that research into MDMA is justified. "Look at heroin. It's a class-A drug that's dangerous when used recreationally, but it's used widely in medicine, and so it should be—it's a very useful drug. Can you imagine saying to the UK [United Kingdom] Royal College of Anaesthetists, 'You can't use morphine or diamorphine [heroin] or pethidine or codeine or any opiate-based drugs because heroin is dangerous and people abuse it?' It's culturally bound. MDMA has been demonized."

In 2004, the most recent year for which there are records, 46 people died after taking Ecstasy, as against 8,221 alcohol-related deaths. And most of those who die with MDMA in their system have mixed it with substances such as alcohol or cannabis, which confounds the picture. . . .

Then there is the problem of funding. MDMA therapy is based on the idea of a single treatment, or a course of treatment sessions, rather than long-term prescriptive use. This presents little or no benefit to drug companies that have huge budgets for research as long as there's a saleable product at the end. And if MDMA does prove effective, companies could stand to lose millions from lost sales of long-term antidepressants prescribed for PTSD.

Sessa says: "There's no financial incentive for the pharmaceutical companies to look into it. Psychotherapy is notoriously underfunded and discredited by the drug companies. It could benefit the government to look into MDMA, but their funding is a drop in the ocean next to a company like Pfizer's research budget. So who's going to pay for a multi-centre psychotherapy trial for 10,000 people—the couch-makers?" . . .

Realistically, would the government ever sanction MDMA research? "It's not impossible, but it's improbable," says Sessa. "It takes a very brave politician to look at the evidence and say, 'Well, there might be positive aspects to this class-A drug. Let's look into it.' It's a conceptual, social battle which won't be easy to win."

TWELVE

Pets Suffer from Anxiety, Too

Carla Hall

> Carla Hall has been a general assignment reporter at *The Los Angeles Times* for fifteen years. Frequently covering animals, she has written numerous articles about both pets and zoo animals—and the people who care for them. In this article Hall discusses the recent trend toward treating animals' anxiety with medication. Many pet owners have been pleased with the results, but pills may not be the quick fix they are looking for.

What could be wrong with Shadow? The green-eyed, long-haired cat had adapted well to his Santa Monica home. There was a carpeted cat tree in the living room for his climbing pleasure. He appeared to have reached an understanding about sharing the house with the other resident feline.

Then one day his owners saw wet spots around the house: Shadow was urine-spraying. The door was a favorite target. So was the side of the sofa. And a corner wall of the living room.

Not to be confused with eschewing [avoiding] the litter pan, spraying is a ritual of territorial marking that cats sometimes do whether they are spayed or neutered—as Shadow is—or not. Shadow's keepers, Fernanda Gray and Elliot Goldberg, were distressed. Pet ownership, they believe, is a trust not to be betrayed.

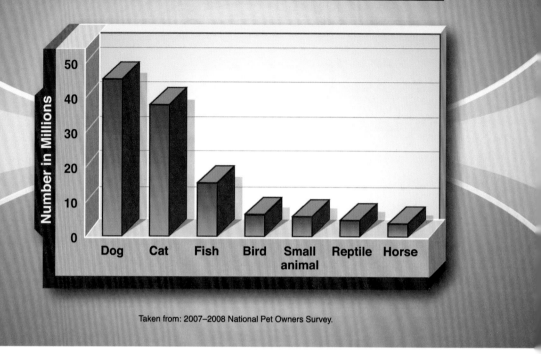

Number of U.S. Households That Own Pets

Number in Millions

Dog	Cat	Fish	Bird	Small animal	Reptile	Horse

Taken from: 2007–2008 National Pet Owners Survey.

"I don't throw animals away," said Gray, who with her husband now owns three cats.

But Shadow's spraying had tested the couple's resolve. They had to replace draperies, carpeting and the sofa. Their veterinarian was running out of ideas to discourage Shadow's habit.

Then Gray saw a small newspaper ad in 2001: "Spraying Cats Needed for Study." Shadow was accepted into a double-blind study of an undisclosed medication's effect on the behavior.

Fourteen days later, the spraying abruptly stopped.

Pets and Antidepressants

The drug was Prozac. Five years later, Shadow is still taking the medication—half a 10-milligram tablet once a day—in its generic form, fluoxetine, a $16 supply of which lasts about four months. "He's still active, he's still his hyperactive self," Gray said. "But it just takes that anxiety away."

They are the new "Prozac Nation": cats, dogs, birds, horses and an assortment of zoo animals whose behavior has been changed, whose anxieties and fears have been quelled and whose owners' furniture has been spared by the use of antidepressants. Over the last decade, Prozac, Buspar, Amitriptyline, Clomicalm—clomipromine that is marketed expressly for dogs—and other drugs have been used to treat inappropriate, destructive and self-injuring behavior in animals.

It's not a big nation yet. But "over the past five years, use has gone up quite a bit," said veterinarian Richard Martin of the Brentwood Pet Clinic in West Los Angeles. Half a decade ago, no more than 1% of his patients were on antidepressants. Now, Martin estimates that 5% of the 8,000 cats and dogs seen at the clinic are taking drugs for their behavior.

The use of antidepressants is another example of the growing sophistication of medical care available to animals and willingly financed by owners who see pets as cherished companions. For these owners, drug therapy is not just another indulgence like Louis Vuitton carriers and day spas for the pampered pet. In their eyes, medication is urgent. Indeed, the new Prozac Nation is not populated with the worried well of the animal kingdom; it's filled with animals behaving so badly they're in danger of being cast off to a shelter and, possibly, a death sentence.

"If you have a cat that sprays constantly, that's not a cat you're likely to keep," said Elyse Kent, the veterinarian who owns the Westside Hospital for Cats. "We were compelled to try these behavioral modification drugs."

Kent has been treating cats with psychoactive drugs, mostly for spraying or aggression, for 12 years. After a UC [University of California at] Davis study published in 2001 showed that fluoxetine reduced feline spraying—and following the success of Kent's patient, Shadow, in a Prozac trial—Prozac became a frequent choice at her clinic. "I'd say twice a week, someone comes in to get a prescription for Prozac or fluoxetine or clomipromine," said Kent, who nonetheless estimates that at any

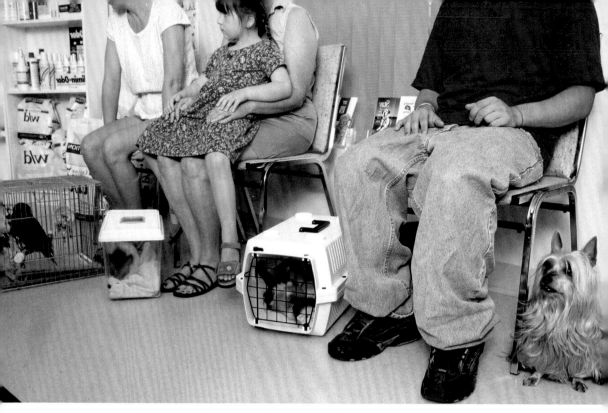

Pets are becoming known as the new "Prozac Nation" because increasing numbers of them are being prescribed antidepressants to quell their anxiety.

one time only 1% of her practice's 3,000 patients are taking a psychoactive drug. ("Six weeks to three months is the average" length of treatment, she said.)

Pills Are Not Always a Quick Fix

Veterinarians who prescribe psychoactive drugs insist they are not Dr. Feelgoods for the animal set. They do medical work-ups on animals, they say, to rule out physical causes for destructive or neurotic actions and prefer to use behavior modification instead of—or, at least, along with—drug therapy. Sometimes they have to deflate the expectations of owners eager to place their pets on antidepressants.

"I tell people if I had a magic pill, I would give it to them," said veterinary behaviorist Karen Sueda, who works at the VCA

West Los Angeles Animal Hospital. "In most cases when we give medication, it is not going to be a quick fix."

Said Curtis Eng, chief veterinarian of the Los Angeles Zoo: "My feeling is they are a useful tool—one of many—to decrease stress and anxiety on an animal. If you can relieve the stressors through a behavior management program, I would much rather do that. But sometimes you need a little extra help to get them over that hump."

When the zoo was coaxing a male orangutan, Minyak, back to respiratory health and enough energy for mating, veterinarians consulted with a psychiatrist and put the primate on the antidepressant Remeron. "He was put on it for depression," said Eng, who noted a beneficial side effect: Minyak hadn't been eating well and the drug increased his appetite. The orangutan bred successfully, fathering a healthy baby in 2005, and he is being weaned off the antidepressant.

The drugs administered to animals fall mainly into two classes of antidepressants commonly prescribed to humans: selective serotonin reuptake inhibitors (SSRIs) and tricyclics. Both groups control the levels in the brain of serotonin, a neurotransmitter that is believed to affect mood, depression and anxiety. The tricyclics also work on other neurotransmitters, including norepinephrine, which is thought to affect attention and impulsiveness.

In most cases, the drugs are being administered off-label, meaning they have not been put through the trials required for FDA approval for use in specific animals. (The Food and Drug Administration [FDA] regulates drugs for both animals and humans.)

Clomicalm, a tricyclic manufactured by Novartis, is the only antidepressant approved by the FDA for dogs as a treatment for separation anxiety. Veterinarian Scott Huggins, manager of technical marketing for Novartis, maker of Clomicalm, said that dogs are not intended to stay on it for life. "We don't have specific studies on long-term use," said Huggins, adding, "I do know it happens."

In general, vets prefer to taper their patients' use of the drugs. "We try to use these medications short-term," said Kent. "Because they are not without side-effects."

Animals Definitely Experience Anxiety

Antidepressants are believed to work on animals' brain chemistry the same way they do on humans'. The difference is that veterinarians will not say they are treating clinical depression; many don't believe an animal can be clinically depressed. "A lot of the outward manifestations—decrease in appetite, trouble sleeping, not taking joy in activities—are there in dogs and cats," Sueda said. "But you can't ask a dog or cat, 'Are you despondent?'"

But veterinarians will say that animals experience anxiety. Dogs with separation anxiety can bark endlessly, destroy household furniture, gnaw through fences or even fling themselves out of windows after owners leave. Birds have compulsively plucked themselves to partial baldness. Troubled cats maul their owners, hide for hours or refuse to use their litter boxes.

Bob Stewart, now the sole owner of a cat since his companion, Anne Marie Schmitt, died of cancer, recalls how his otherwise mellow feline would turn into a leopard-like creature. At one point, when Serendipity clawed Schmitt's arm badly enough to send her to the hospital, Stewart says they considered drastic action. "If we could not have gotten her controlled, as much as we loved the cat, we probably would have had to find a way to get her adopted or send her to one of these shelters," said Stewart, a retired game show producer who created the original "The Price Is Right" and "Password."

The owners refused to have the cat declawed. Instead, for the last several years, a daily dose of "triple fish-flavored" fluoxetine has, for the most part, quashed Serendipity's desire to practice her hunting skills on humans. "I thought it made sense," said Stewart, sitting in his apartment with Serendipity resting nearby. "They feel pain as we feel pain. They feel happiness as we feel happiness. I didn't question the idea that a drug could change the persona of an animal."

Treatment by Trial and Error

As with humans, choosing the right drug and dosage for an animal is a process of trial-and-error. "A lot of behavior treatment is an art," Sueda said.

No one knows that better than Amy Weber, who adopted Sam, a spayed female dog, 10 years ago. The Labrador/beagle mix appears sweet-natured and calm as she lies in the living room of the rambling Beechwood Canyon home Weber shares with her partner, Wendy Schwartz, and five pets. The couple's other dog, Scout, busily scouts for affection. A hulking orange cat, Stripper, saunters by, pausing to swat Sam. The action elicits a gasp from the humans but only a quizzical look from Sam.

For several years, Sam was anything but calm when her owners left the house. She scratched doors, chewed through washing machine hoses and gnawed the wood trim on windows, sometimes cutting her mouth. If she was left outside, she either dug her way out of the yard or ripped through wire fences, scratching her head in the process.

Weber tried Clomicalm, tranquilizers, homeopathic remedies and Cesar Millan, the "Dog Whisperer." But Sam's separation anxiety defied all drugs and therapy for a time. Although Weber, who edits movie trailers, put together a nearly full-time schedule of sitters and walkers for Sam, that didn't stop the dog from going into a frenzy if Weber and Schwartz went out for the evening.

Then Weber hired Sueda, who put Sam on a regimen of Amitriptyline during the day and recommended Xanax at night if the couple wanted to go out. And she started the dog and her owners on a behavior training program. . . . "I never look at medication as a cure-all—just like with people," said the veterinarian, who delves into the history of each animal's situation.

Appointments with Sueda aren't cheap. A package of two lengthy visits—the first is two hours—follow-up phone calls and e-mails is $550, not counting what Sueda charges if she travels to the owner's house.

Brand-name Prozac can cost more than $100 a month, but most vets now prescribe fluoxetine, a monthly regimen of which can cost pet owners a few dollars a month to about $20, depending on the dosage.

Alternative Treatments

[Melissa] Bain [chief of behavior service at UC Davis School of Veterinary Medicine] is wary of medications. "Drugs don't work that easily," she said. "And they don't work with behavior modification."

Much of what animals do, Bain said, is normal, just unacceptable—a result of owners incorporating their pets into close urban quarters. "Breeds of animals have not changed that much in 20 or 30 years, but human society has," she said. "What have we done to our animals? In the last 30 years, we've kept them inside, we've made multiple-cat households. A border collie, 20 years ago, was living on a ranch in Colorado, and now he's living in downtown San Francisco. So he can't do his typical behavior."

Moustafa Seoud, a veterinarian for 17 years, sees drugs like Clomicalm or Prozac as "an easy way out." Seoud, who practices at the Laurel Pet Hospital in West Hollywood [California], relies on massage, acupuncture and homeopathic treatments. "Homeopathic flower essence works well for cats with different problems—stress and anxiety and kidney problems."

He dispenses different types of remedies for different problems: "Camomile is calming; Ignatia for grieving; Nux Vomica for nervousness." One of Seoud's clients said that one time, as he prescribed a homeopathic remedy for her withdrawn cat, he popped some of it into his own mouth and declared: "You can take it too."

Conventional drugs seem to be working for Sam, the dog with the bad case of separation anxiety. Weber tells Sueda that Sam has been fine when she's left the dog alone for a few hours during the day. And Sam has stopped following Weber around the house constantly. "She's just calmer," Weber said.

"That's what we're aiming for," Sueda said. "A general, overall sense of calm."

THIRTEEN

One Teen's Struggle to Overcome Anxiety

Good Morning America

> *Good Morning America* is an Emmy-winning news and talk show that airs daily on ABC. This story follows one teenage girl's struggle with anxiety. Lindsay Lanouette had suffered panic attacks her entire life. When she was in high school, anxiety limited her academically and socially. Lanouette went through a five-day intensive treatment program that helped alleviate her symptoms and allowed her to do things she previously would have been too panic-stricken to try.

There are thousands of known and studied phobias from aulophobia, a fear of flutes; to xanthophobia, a fear of the color yellow.

"We had somebody who was deathly afraid of people hiccupping," said Dr. David Barlow of the Center for Anxiety and Related Disorders at Boston University. "They would not put themselves in a situation where they might be around someone who would be likely to hiccup."

If a person knows what their fear is, they know how to avoid it. But for more than six million Americans with panic disorder, they can never be sure what will spark their fear or when it will come over them.

Lindsay Lanouette is the last person you'd think has any reason for fear or worry. The 16-year-old from Falmouth, Maine, is a great athlete, gets good grades and has many friends. "Sometimes I have the fear of like—that I'm gonna like die," she said. "I guess, like, cause, I won't be able to get help."

But her panic attacks can set in at any time. You can see it happening in English class when her legs begin to shake uncontrollably. "I'm always, like, constantly moving my legs," Lindsay said. "I don't even know if it's like a nervous habit."

Her panic might arise during gym class, when her heart started beating faster. "My heart kind of starts racing a little bit, I just get really nervous," she said.

Outside the familiar confines of school, her symptoms are even worse. "When I go to the mall by myself, generally, it's like I get kind of dizzy," Lindsay said.

Lifelong Struggle

Lindsay's parents say she's been struggling with panic her entire life. "Initially, it was just some separation problems with going to daycare or kindergarten," said Kathy Lanouette, Lindsay's mother.

"She'll say that her hands are tingly, her feet are tingly, she feels separated from her body," said Jason Lanouette, Lindsay's father. Up until now, the family has tried to cope by keeping Lindsay out of places where she panics, like restaurants and movie theatres. But they can't protect her forever. She's almost old enough to go to college.

"I just worry about—sometimes because I think sometimes she feels really bad that she has this and doesn't understand it," said Kathy Lanouette. "I just worry about some of the thoughts that she has said before—you know, that she doesn't want to live anymore."

Recently, the family received new hope. A friend told the Lanouettes about the Center for Anxiety and Related Disorders, located two hours away at Boston University. The center offers a five-day intensive treatment program for adolescents like Lindsay. Dr. Donna Pincus helped lead her through it.

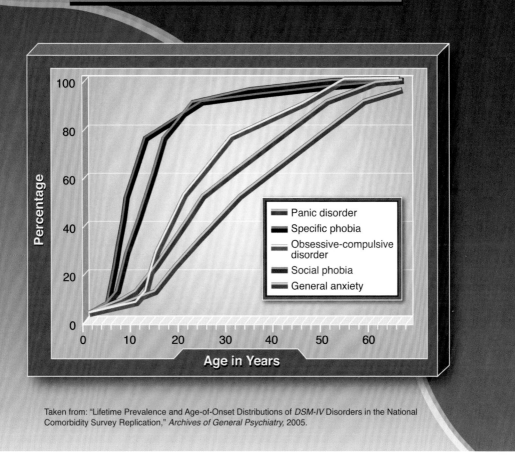

Age by Which Anxiety Sufferers First Experience Symptoms

Panic disorder
Specific phobia
Obsessive-compulsive disorder
Social phobia
General anxiety

Percentage

Age in Years

Taken from: "Lifetime Prevalence and Age-of-Onset Distributions of *DSM-IV* Disorders in the National Comorbidity Survey Replication," *Archives of General Psychiatry,* 2005.

"I'd like you to just almost be like a scientist with me," Pincus told Lindsay. "I want us to watch what happens and I want us to watch what happens right before you have a panic attack."

Doctors are still studying what causes panic disorder. One theory is that it has to do with the amygdala, the part of the brain that coordinates the body's automatic response to fear. Perhaps it activates too frequently in certain people. "What we have to do together is teach that watchdog in your brain to not bark so much at times when there's not really any danger there," Pincus told Lindsay during one of their sessions.

Facing Her Fears

Pincus and other doctors at the center placed Lindsay in the very situations that cause her the most panic.

Days one and two of Lindsay's five-day treatment are devoted to psychotherapy. Pincus wants to train her not to run for help when her panic attacks set in. "The more you avoid and decide, 'Okay,

A short period of intensive psychotherapy can help individuals with anixety disorders confront their fears and learn coping skills to help eliminate them.

I'm not gonna stay at school and I'm not gonna stay in my bed at night,' what do you think happens to your panic thoughts?" Pincus said to Lindsay during one of their sessions. "The next time you get into your bed at night, do you think it will be easier or harder?"

"Harder," Lindsay said.

"Yeah, and do you think those panic thoughts might be even stronger," Pincus said.

"Yeah," Lindsay said.

Pincus told Lindsay that she needs to experience her feelings of anxiety in order to overcome them. She puts Lindsay through a series of exercises designed to produce the physical sensations that normally accompany her panic attack: jogging in place to make her heart race; breathing through a cocktail straw to make her feel faint; staring at a bright light bulb, which makes her leg start to shake uncontrollably. "Our goal is going to be to continue to experience these feelings and allow the body to resolve itself," Pincus said.

Pincus has Lindsay's parents go through the exercises so they understand what their daughter feels like every day.

On day four, it was time for Lindsay to try it in the real world. Pincus loaded Lindsay up with caffeine to make her jittery. She took away Lindsay's cell phone and iPod and sent her off on the Boston subway alone. The fear set in quickly. "I was just like nervous," Lindsay said. "I had a headache."

The next assignment prompted a full-blown panic attack. As Lindsay got her food and sat alone, her anxiety level climbed to what she estimates is a seven on an eight-point scale. But she stayed put and rode the wave of panic until it subsided. Pincus said it was a breakthrough.

On day five, Pincus put Lindsay through her toughest trial yet and sent her on a 90-minute boat tour with no way to escape and no one she knew aboard to turn to if she panicked, but she made it.

Feeling Better

"I'm just really excited," Lindsay said. "I mean, we waited a long time for this and you know, I can already feel the difference."

"I think Lindsay has done incredibly well and gotten herself to a point where now, if she continues practicing, she will be cured," Pincus said.

Lindsay came so far that she was able to attend a Jason Mraz concert. Concerts used to bring out intense feelings of anxiety. "It was really good," Lindsay said. "Today it was easy. I'm planning to go to more concerts and do more things on my own."

What You Should Know About Anxiety Disorders

Facts About Anxiety Disorders

- More than 40 million Americans suffer from anxiety disorders.
- Anxiety disorders were first officially recognized in the *Diagnostic and Statistical Manual of Mental Disorders III (DSM-III)* in 1980.
- Women are twice as likely as men to suffer from generalized anxiety disorder, panic disorder, post-traumatic stress disorder, and specific phobias.
- People with an anxiety disorder are three to five times more likely to go to the doctor and six times more likely to be hospitalized for psychiatric disorders than those who do not suffer from anxiety disorders.
- Most people with one anxiety disorder will also have another anxiety disorder.
- People with obsessive-compulsive disorder (OCD) know their obsessions and compulsions are irrational and excessive, yet have little to no control over them.
- OCD sufferers obsessively repeat certain behaviors. Some of the more common of these behaviors are repeating words or phrases, hoarding, putting things in order, hand washing, counting, tapping, and checking things such as the stove or door locks.
- Compulsive gambling, eating, and addiction are *not* categorized as OCD.
- People with social phobia are less likely to have full-time employment.

- Each year social anxiety disorder affects approximately 15 million American adults, with nearly 7 percent suffering from the disorder in any given year and approximately 12 percent afflicted at some point in their lifetime.
- Social phobia typically develops in childhood or adolescence.
- Almost two-thirds of those diagnosed with generalized anxiety disorder (GAD) will suffer from depression.
- Sufferers of GAD have severe, continuous tension that interferes with their daily lives.
- About one-third of those with generalized anxiety disorder will have problems with drug or alcohol abuse.
- GAD may cause physical symptoms, including a rapid heart rate, difficulty breathing, dry mouth, and dizziness.
- Victims of panic disorder suffer panic attacks, which are sudden attacks of terror, accompanied by such physical symptoms as faintness, weakness, lightheadedness, excessive sweating, increased heart rate, chest pain, nausea, numbness, and shaking.
- One-third of panic attack sufferers develops agoraphobia. Agoraphobia is the fear of being anywhere it would be difficult to escape or receive help in the event of a panic attack.
- About one-fifth of Vietnam veterans experienced post-traumatic stress disorder (PTSD). Similar rates are being reported in veterans returning from Afghanistan and Iraq.
- PTSD may occur shortly after the traumatic event that caused it. In other cases, symptoms may not appear until many years after the event.
- A political debate is currently under way over what degree of treatment for PTSD in veterans should be made available—and paid for—by the government.
- Specific phobias often manifest in childhood; the median age of onset is seven.
- Some of the more common specific phobias include the following: water, flying, needles, closed spaces, heights, animals (particularly rodents, reptiles, bugs, or spiders), bridges, and tunnels.

Facts About Treatment

- Psychiatric treatment of all anxiety disorders costs approximately $13.3 billion a year in the United States.
- Cognitive-behavioral therapy (CBT) is often used to treat anxiety disorders. CBT is a treatment method that focuses on thought patterns and on responses to triggering situations. It teaches techniques for dealing with anxiety and stress.
- Phobias and OCD can be treated with exposure therapy: gradually exposing patients to the subjects of their fears while teaching them relaxation techniques until they are confronting their fears head-on.
- Meditation and acupuncture are used to treat anxiety.
- Herbal remedies reputed to treat anxiety include Saint John's wort, chamomile, kava, and marijuana.
- Leading antianxiety medications include Effexor, Zoloft, Paxil, Lexapro, Cymbalta, Prozac, and Anafranil.

What You Should Do About Anxiety Disorders

A nxiety disorders affect millions of people in America. The conditions have been around for centuries but are only recently becoming recognized as the legitimate health problems that they are. These disorders can be treated, and in most cases many options for doing so are available. However, a lack of understanding about the disorders and a stigma against having a mental illness prevent many cases from ever getting diagnosed and treated. When left untreated, anxiety disorders can worsen and lead to other health problems such as depression and substance abuse.

The more society understands about anxiety disorders and accepts that they are harmful conditions, the less devastation the disorders will have on the lives of people who suffer from them.

Gather Information on Conditions and Symptoms

Anxiety disorders can take many forms, and while they all share certain features, each has its own unique characteristics. Since anxiety disorders were officially classified in 1980, awareness of the problem has grown. Now many organizations are eager to provide detailed information about the conditions in efforts to further raise awareness. Many such organizations are listed in the Organizations to Contact section of this book. Most have detailed information available online and additional brochures or packets available upon request and are eager to respond to your questions about anxiety disorders.

Many articles about anxiety disorders—including some articles listed in the bibliography—contain personal stories about the struggles of coping with these conditions. You may be able to obtain additional information through personal interviews. Perhaps you know someone who has an anxiety disorder and is willing to share his or her experience. Many advocates for organizations devoted to anxiety disorders have overcome, or continue to deal with, anxiety problems and will share their stories to raise awareness.

Understand Treatment Options

Today, many treatments for anxiety disorders are available. Different treatment options may be better suited for different people, depending on the nature, degree, and cause of the disorder. With the guidance of a parent or other trusted adult, contact doctors, therapists, and treatment centers for more information on treatment options. Manufacturers of medications also provide information about their products and how they work. Do keep in mind that pharmaceutical companies are competing to sell their drugs and thus have financial incentives to promote their medications. This applies to for-profit treatment centers as well. Always consider your source—and its motives—when evaluating the information you receive.

Know the Resources Available to Students

As students, you will often have additional resources available beyond those accessible to the general public. While in high school, you can contact your school's health or counseling office for information on dealing with anxiety as a teenager. Many anxiety disorders begin during adolescence, and high school personnel are trained to deal with them. Additional resources are also available should you move on to college. The transition to college is inevitably a stressful time, and many campuses offer support for incoming students. Many schools recognize the unique pressures facing university students and have resources on campus to help these students cope. Students can contact campus health centers, in person or online, to receive information and strategies for coping with anxiety caused by the pressures of college life. Counselors are also available for those students who need their services.

Anxiety disorders affect millions of Americans. Awareness of this issue is growing. As it does, researchers may discover more about the causes and symptoms of the disorders. New treatment methods may be developed and old methods refined. Starting with this book, and continuing beyond as your research expands, you can understand the history and many facets of this prevalent issue.

ORGANIZATIONS TO CONTACT

The editors have compiled the following list of organizations concerned with the issues debated in this book. The descriptions are derived from materials provided by the organizations. All have publications or information available for interested readers. The list was compiled on the date of publication of the present volume; the information provided here may change. Be aware that many organizations take several weeks or longer to respond to inquiries, so allow as much time as possible.

Active Minds
2647 Connecticut Ave. NW, Ste. 200, Washington, DC 20008
(202) 332-9595
e-mail: info@activeminds.org
Web site: www.activeminds.org

Active Minds is working to utilize the student voice to change the conversation about mental health on college campuses. By developing and supporting chapters of a student-run mental health awareness, education, and advocacy group on campuses, the organization works to increase students' awareness of mental health issues, provide information and resources regarding mental health and mental illness, encourage students to seek help as soon as it is needed, and serve as liaison between students and the mental health community.

American Psychiatric Association (APA)
APA Answer Center
1000 Wilson Blvd., Ste. 1825, Arlington, VA 22209
(888) 357-7924
e-mail: apa@psych.org
Web site: www.healthyminds.org

The APA is a national medical specialty society whose physician members specialize in diagnosis, treatment, prevention, and research of mental illnesses. HealthyMinds.org is the APA's online resource for anyone seeking mental health information. It provides information on many common mental health concerns, including warning signs of mental disorders, treatment options, and preventative measures.

Anxiety Disorders Association of America (ADAA)
8730 Georgia Ave., Ste. 600, Silver Spring, MD 20910
(240) 485-1001
e-mail: information@adaa.org
Web site: www.aada.org

ADAA is a national nonprofit organization dedicated to the prevention, treatment, and cure of anxiety disorders and to improving the lives of all people who suffer from them. The association is made up of professionals who conduct research and treat anxiety disorders, and of people who have personal or general interests in learning more about anxiety disorders. ADAA disseminates information, links people who need treatment with those who can provide it, and advocates for cost-effective treatments.

Anxiety Disorders Association of Canada (ADAC/ACTA)
PO Box 117, Station Cote St-Luc, Montreal, QC H4V 2Y3
(888) 223-2252
e-mail: contactus@anxietycanada.ca
Web site: www.anxietycanada.ca

ADAC—known in French as the Association Canadienne des Troubles Anxieux (ACTA)—is a Canadian nonprofit organization whose aim is to promote the prevention, treatment, and management of anxiety disorders and to improve the lives of people who suffer from them. The organization seeks to educate consumers, professionals, and the public at large about anxiety disorders so that informed treatment choices can be made.

Association for Behavioral and Cognitive Therapies (ABCT)
305 Seventh Ave., 16th Fl., New York, NY 10001
(212) 647-1890
Web site: www.abct.org

The ABCT is an interdisciplinary organization committed to the advancement of a scientific approach to the understanding and improvement of problems of the human condition. These aims are achieved through the investigation and application of behavioral, cognitive, and other evidence-based principles to assessment, prevention, and treatment. The organization's Web site offers information about symptoms, treatments, providers, and employment opportunities.

Give an Hour
PO Box 5918, Bethesda, MD 20824-5918
e-mail: info@giveanhour.org
Web site: www.giveanhour.org

Give an Hour is a nonprofit organization whose mission is to develop national networks of volunteers capable of responding to both acute and chronic conditions that arise within society. Currently, Give an Hour is dedicated to meeting the mental health needs of the troops and families affected by the ongoing conflicts in Iraq and Afghanistan, many of whom suffer from post-traumatic stress disorder, depression, and anxiety.

The Mayo Clinic
200 First St. SW, Rochester, MN 55905
e-mail: mayoinfo@mayoclinic.com
Web site: www.mayoclinic.com

Owned by the Mayo Foundation for Medical Education and Research, Mayoclinic.com provides up-to-date information and tools for understanding medical problems, conditions, and treatment. Thousands of medical professionals contribute to the site, which contains detailed information about the causes, symptoms, and treatments of various anxiety disorders.

Mental Health America (MHA)
2000 N. Beauregard St., 6th Fl., Alexandria, VA 22311
(703) 684-7722
Web site: www.mentalhealthamerica.nct

MHA, formerly known as the National Mental Health Association, is a nonprofit organization dedicated to helping all people live mentally healthier lives. With more than 320 affiliates nationwide, MHA promotes the mental well-being of the nation, both daily and in times of crisis. MHA promotes education, research, and policy to raise awareness and assist those suffering from mental illness.

National Alliance on Mental Illness (NAMI)
Colonial Place Three, 2107 Wilson Blvd., Ste. 300, Arlington, VA 22201-3042
(703) 524-7600
Web site: www.nami.org

NAMI is a grassroots organization for people with mental illness and their families. Founded in 1979, NAMI has affiliates in every state and in more than eleven hundred local communities across the country. The alliance is dedicated to the eradication of mental illnesses and to the improvement of the quality of life through support, education, and advocacy for persons of all ages who are affected by mental illnesses.

National Center for PTSD
(802) 296-6300
e-mail: ncptsd@va.gov
Web site: www.ptsd.va.gov

Run by the Department of Veterans Affairs, the National Center for PTSD (post-traumatic stress disorder) focuses on research and education about the prevention, understanding, and treatment of PTSD. The center has seven divisions across the country. Although the center provides no direct clinical care, its purpose is to improve the well-being and understanding of American veterans.

National Institute of Mental Health (NIMH)
6001 Executive Blvd., Rm. 8184, MSC 9663, Bethesda, MD 20892-9663
(866) 615-6464
e-mail: nimhinfo@nih.gov
Web site: www.nimh.nih.gov

The NIMH is a scientific organization dedicated to research focused on mental disorders and the promotion of mental health. Its mission is to transform the understanding and treatment of mental illnesses through research, paving the way for prevention, recovery, and cure.

The Obsessive Compulsive Foundation (OCF)
PO Box 961029, Boston, MA 02196
(617) 973-5801
e-mail: info@ocfoundation.org
Web site: www.ocfoundation.org

The OCF is an international not-for-profit organization composed of people with obsessive-compulsive disorder (OCD) and related disorders, their families, friends, professionals, and other concerned individuals. The OCF was founded in 1986 by a group of individuals with OCD, and its mission is to educate the public and professional communities about OCD and related disorders; to provide assistance to individuals with OCD and related disorders and to their families and friends; and to support research into the causes and effective treatments of OCD and related disorders. OCF also runs a webzine—*Organized Chaos*—specifically for adolescents with OCD.

Psych Central
55 Pleasant St., Ste. 207, Newburyport, MA 01950
(978) 992-0008
e-mail: talkback@psychcentral.com
Web site: www.psychcentral.com

Psych Central is an independent online mental health social network created and run by mental health professionals. It is an online information source for mental health information and provides guides to Web sites, newsgroups, and mailing lists online in mental health, psychology, social work, and psychiatry. It also developed the Sanity Score, a free online mental health screening test.

World Federation for Mental Health (WFMH)
12940 Harbor Dr., Ste. 101, Woodbridge, VA 22192
(703) 494-6515
e-mail: info@wfmh.org
Web site: www.wfmh.org

WFMH is an international membership organization founded in 1948 to advance the prevention of mental and emotional disorders, the proper treatment and care of those with such disorders, and the promotion of mental health. The federation, through its members and contacts in more than one hundred countries on six continents, has responded to international mental health crises through its role as a worldwide grassroots advocacy and public education organization in the mental health field. Its organizational and individual memberships include mental health workers of all disciplines, consumers of mental health services, family members, and concerned citizens.

BIBLIOGRAPHY

Books

Art Bell, *Phobias and How to Overcome Them: Understanding and Beating Your Fears*. Franklin Lakes, NJ: Career Press, 2008.

Jeff Bell, *Rewind, Replay, Repeat: A Memoir of Obsessive-Compulsive Disorder*. Center City, MN: Hazelden, 2007.

Ronald M. Doctor, Ada P. Kahn, and Christine Adamec, *The Encyclopedia of Phobias, Fears, and Anxieties*. New York: Facts On File, 2008.

Emily Ford, Michael Liebowitz, and Linda Wasmer Andrews, *What You Must Think of Me: A Firsthand Account of One Teenager's Experience with Social Anxiety Disorder*. New York: Oxford University Press, 2007.

David Herzberg, *Happy Pills in America: From Miltown to Prozac*. Baltimore: Johns Hopkins University Press, 2008.

Muriel K. MacFarlane, *Panic Attack, Anxiety and Phobia Solutions Handbook*. Oak Lawn, IL: Atlantic, 2008.

Ian Osborn, *Tormenting Thoughts and Secret Rituals: The Hidden Epidemic of Obsessive-Compulsive Disorder*. New York: Dell, 1999.

Patricia Pearson, *A Brief History of Anxiety (Yours and Mine)*. East Mississauga, ON: Random House Canada, 2008.

Andrea Perry, *Claustrophobia*. New York: Worth, 2007.

Reneau Z. Peurifoy, *Anxiety, Phobias, and Panic*. New York: Grand Central, 2005.

Christina Hoff Sommers, *One Nation Under Therapy: How the Helping Culture Is Eroding Self-Reliance*. New York: St. Martin's Griffin, 2006.

Edward Tick, *War and the Soul: Healing Our Nation's Veterans from Post-traumatic Stress Disorder*. Burlington, ON: Quest, 2005.

David F. Tolin, Randy O. Frost, and Gail Steketee, *Buried in Treasures: Help for Compulsive Acquiring, Saving, and Hoarding.* New York: Oxford University Press, 2007.

Andrea Tone, *The Age of Anxiety: A History of America's Turbulent Affair with Tranquilizers.* New York: Basic Books, 2008.

Richard Waters, *Phobias: Revealed and Explained.* Hauppauge, NY: Barron's Educational Series, 2003.

Rebecca Woolis, *When Someone You Love Has a Mental Illness.* New York: Penguin, 2003.

Periodicals and Internet Sources

Lisa Belkin, "Can You Catch Obsessive-Compulsive Disorder?" *New York Times*, May 22, 2005.

Lauren Cox, "Needle Phobia More Common than Many Believe," ABC News, January 2, 2008. http://abcnews.go.com.

Kathleen Doheny, "Healthy Traveler; Loosening the Grip of Separation Anxiety," *Los Angeles Times*, May 11, 2003.

Kassidy Emmerson, "The Ten Most Common Phobias: Do You Suffer from Any of These Fears?" Associated Content, April 23, 2007. www.associatedcontent.com.

Frontline, "A Soldier's Heart: Interview with Thomas Burk," PBS, December 28, 2004. www.pbs.org.

A. Chris Gajilan, "Iraq Vets and Post-traumatic Stress: No Easy Answers," CNN Health, October 24, 2008. www.cnnhealth.com.

Amanda Gardner, "Anxiety Rising on U.S. College Campuses," *Washington Post*, March 27, 2007.

Good Morning America, "The Face of OCD," ABC News, April 10, 2006. http://abcnews.go.com.

Susan Donaldson James, "Not So Vain: Carly Simon's Panicky Past," ABC News, April 30, 2008. http://abcnews.go.com.

Barbara Kantrowitz and Pat Wingert, "Help for Panic Attacks," *Newsweek*, June 25, 2008.

Wayne Katon and Peter Roy-Byrne, "Anxiety Disorders: Efficient Screening Is the First Step in Improving Outcomes," *Annals of Internal Medicine*, March 6, 2007.

Susan Kinzie, "Orientation 101 for Parents and Freshmen: Letting Go," *Washington Post*, August 26, 2007.

G. Jeffery MacDonald, "Parents of College Freshmen Feel Separation Anxiety," *USA Today*, September 12, 2007.

Jeff Minerd, "USPSYCH: 'Katrina Brain' Pervasive After Hurricane," *Psychiatric Times*, November 22, 2006.

Adele Slaughter and Stephen A. Shoop, "Shaloub Brings Obsessive Compulsive Disorder to Light," *USA Today*, August 20, 2002.

INDEX

PICTURE CREDITS

Maury Aaseng, 17, 22, 26, 31, 34, 41, 47, 55, 57, 68, 77, 80, 89

AJPhoto/Hôpital de Pédiatrie et de Rééducation de Bullion/Photo Researchers, Inc., 20, 25

AJPhoto/Photo Researchers, Inc., 90

AP Images, 7, 52

© Bubbles Photolibrary/Alamy, 29

Carolyn A. McKeone/Photo Researchers, Inc., 82

Charles Ommanney/Getty Images, 72

Cristina Pedrazzini/Photo Researchers, Inc., 48

Phanie/Photo Researchers, Inc., 11

Joe Raedle/Getty Images, 66

Susan Rosenberg/Photo Researchers, Inc., 39

Paul Thompson/FPG/Getty Images, 60

© Carol and Mike Werner/PHOTOTAKE/Alamy, 36